THE INTERPRETATION
OF THE KORAN
IN MODERN EGYPT

THE INTERPRETATION
OF THE KORAN
IN MODERN EGYPT

BY

J. J. G. JANSEN

LEIDEN
E. J. BRILL
1974

Dissertatie Leiden 1974

ISBN   90 04 04009 9

THE INTERPRETATION
OF THE KORAN
IN MODERN EGYPT

BY

J. J. G. JANSEN

LEIDEN
E. J. BRILL
1974

CONTENTS

PREFACE

In 1966/67 I had the opportunity to spend a year in Cairo on an Egyptian-Dutch exchange scholarship. When visiting the book-shops of that city I was invariably struck by the large quantities of old and modern Koran commentaries which Egyptian publishing houses have offered to the public in the last decades, and by the wide public interest in these works. Moreover, many of the modern commentaries were not mentioned or discussed in the extant Western works on Koran exegesis and its history. When I saw the Koran commentary by Dr. 'Â'isha 'Abd ar-Rahmân Bint as-Shâti', the first woman ever to write a commentary on the Koran, it occurred to me that modern Egyptian Koran interpretation might deserve more attention than it has received up to the present.

The two most important Western works on modern Moslem Koran interpretation are Dr. J. Jomier's *Le commentaire Coranique du Manâr* (1954) and Dr. J. M. S. Baljon's *Modern Muslim Koran Interpretation* (1961). Dr. Jomier's book exclusively treats of the Koran commentary by Mohammed Abduh (d. 1905) and Rashîd Ridâ (d. 1935). It offers a virtually complete synopsis of everything which these two reformers taught. For this exposé, Dr. Jomier naturally consulted other sources as well. Dr. Baljon's book has the merit of also discussing Urdu commentaries. Regrettably, however, the Koran commentaries by Bint as-Shâti' had not yet appeared at the time Dr. Baljon wrote his study. In consequence, his book seems to pay too little attention to Koran interpretation and philology.

Both books, moreover, have a more or less double aim. They give a picture of modern Islam as seen through the modern Koran commentaries, and, at the same time, they give the Western reader an idea of what modern Koran commentaries look like. These two aims may not be incompatible, but there is little reason to base a description of modern Islam on sources of one kind (e.g. Koran commentaries) exclusively. Both books, being more concerned with Islam than with Koran commentaries, pay little attention to the methods (not to use a pejorative like "tricks") which the modern exegetes employ in order to reach their—often apologetic—aims. Also both books give the impression that contemporary Koran commentaries and commentaries written before the nineteenth century are a different thing altogether. This is only partially true. Modern commentaries are written for another public than the "classical" commentaries, but they are still very much traditional in contents and form.

To the Western reader a Koran commentary is something mysterious. In order to mitigate the severity of this mysteriousness, an attempt to classify contemporary commentaries would be welcome. However, any attempt at classification is bound to receive criticism as to the criterion which is used, whether it be period, tendency or form. One of the most eloquent critics of "classification", the English novelist E. M. Forster, in his *Aspects of the Novel*, effectively derides the pseudo-scientific attempts at dividing literature into periods: "Books written before 1847, books written after it, books written after or before 1848."[1] According to E. M. Forster, the first crime of the pseudo-scholar is classification by chronology.

But classification by tendency also evokes his mockery: "As soon as he [E. M. Forster's "pseudo-scholar"] can use the word 'tendency' his spirits rise, and though those of his audience may sink, they often pull out their pencils at this point and make a note, under the belief that a tendency is portable."[2] Writers about Koran exegesis may profit from Forster's warning. It would be most attractive to be able to divide the mass of Koran commentaries into a number of groups according to their tendency. Such a clear-cut division according to tendencies, however, is falsified by the mixed nature of the contents of most commentaries. Far from being dedicated to any one tendency, modern Egyptian Koran commentaries usually consist of remarks concerning the philology of the Koran; remarks concerning the Koran and natural history; and, thirdly, remarks on the Koran and how people should act in this world.

E. M. Forster wants us to visualize all writers as "seated together in a room, a circular room, a sort of British Museum reading room—all writing their [books] simultaneously."[3] Forster, writing about novels and not about Koran commentaries, then suggests talking about the *aspects* of the novel, because, as Forster puts it,

---

[1] E. M. Forster, *Aspects of the Novel*, 19.
[2] ib., 21.
[3] ib., 16.

this term is sufficiently vague, and because it means both the different ways a writer can look at his works and the different ways we can look at them.

It is dangerous to adopt Forster's simile while describing the activities of the Egyptian contemporary interpreters of the Koran. It is, however, tempting to imagine them too as all working together in one large circular reading room. In this imaginary Cairo reading room, they perceive the Koran from three viewpoints. These points of view are philology, natural history, and the day-to-day affairs of the Moslems in this world. The enigmatic Mohammed Abduh has great influence on all present in this reading room. An attempt at working out this metaphor will be offered in the following chapters.[4]

---

[4] When the present work was nearly finished, I came across a book by Dr. I. M. As-Sharqâwî, *Ittigâhât at-Tafsîr fî Misr fî-l-ʿAsr al-Hadîth* (Cairo 1972). In this book Dr. As-Sharqâwî has not incorporated publications which appeared after 1963. Also he makes use of unpublished manuscripts on Koran exegesis (e.g. p. 313) whereas there seems to be no lack of published Koran commentaries. His judgement on Bint as-Shâtiʾ is not favourable (p. 323). Dr. As-Sharqâwî discerns three tendencies in modern Egyptian Koran interpretation: *al-ittigâh al-igtimâʿî* (p. 89), *al-ittigâh al-adabî* (p. 269) and *al-ittigâh al-ʿilmî* (p. 389).

ACKNOWLEDGEMENTS

I am greatly indebted to Mr. J. van der Walle, of Brill Leiden, who spared no effort to supply me with the books I needed. Thanks to his untiring work, I acquired books which would otherwise have remained unknown to me.

Many others have helped and encouraged me. From these pages I thank and salute them.

Finally, I am indebted to the Netherlands Organization for the Advancement of Pure Research (Z.W.O.), which enabled me to collect material for my studies in Egypt.

Leiden, December 1973   J. J. G. JANSEN

ABBREVIATIONS

EI   *Encyclopaedia of Islam.*
GAL   C. Brockelmann, *Geschichte der Arabischen Litteratur²*.
GdQ   Th. Nöldeke a.o., *Geschichte des Qorâns²*.
GAS   F. Sezgin, *Geschichte des Arabischen Schrifttums.*
MIDEO   *Mélanges de l'Institut Dominicain d'Etudes Orientales du Caire.*

NOTE ON THE TRANSCRIPTION OF ARABIC WORDS

â, '	ا	*d*	د	*d*	ض	*k*	ك
b	ب	*dh*	ذ	*t*	ط	*l*	ل
t	ت	*r*	ر	*z*	ظ	*m*	م
th	ث	*z*	ز	'	ع	*n*	ن
g	ج	*s*	س	*gh*	غ	*h*	ه
h	ح	*sh*	ش	*f*	ف	*û, w*	و
kh	خ	*s*	ص	*q*	ق	*î, y*	ى

In genitive constructions (Ar.: *idâfa*) the *tâ' marbûta* is transcribed as *t*; otherwise it is not transcribed.

The Prophet's name is transcribed as *Mohammed*. Likewise: Mohammed Abduh, Caliph, Koran, Mecca, Moslem, Mutazilite, Sura, etc. Nevertheless, less eminent persons bearing the Prophet's name are called *Muhammad*.

The words "Tradition" and "Traditional", with a capital letter, refer to *hadîth*, "a Tradition traced up to Mohammed". Written without capital, these words retain their usual sense.

CHAPTER ONE

INTRODUCTION

THE KORAN AND ITS INTERPRETATION

Many sayings have been attributed to Mohammed, the Prophet
of Islam. After his death these sayings have been included in the
famous collections of Traditions on the life of Mohammed and his
contemporaries. One of the most important of these collections, the
so-called *Al-Gâmiʿ as-Sahîh* of Al-Bukhârî, contains several thou-
sands.[1] Already in the days of Mohammed these ordinary sayings
were apparently discernible from certain other utterances of
Mohammed, utterances that were thought to be divine: not orig-
inating from Mohammed himself, but given to him by God, in
dreams, in visions, by means of the Angel Gabriel, in states of
religious extasy and otherwise. These supposedly divine utterances
were later on to be collected in the Koran.[2]

The Koran is the very word of God, as all Moslems have believed
throughout the ages. Taken literally, this proposition has implications that become evident when one makes a comparison with the
Christian view of the four Gospels. Their four writers are known
by name: Mark, Matthew, Luke and John. Each of them wrote in
his own words for his own public an account of the divine happen-
ings in the days of Christ. Not so the Koran; its author is not
Mohammed, who tells in his own words, though heavenly inspired,
about his spiritual intercourse with God. It is God himself who is
assumed to be speaking, making statements about himself, occasionally even speaking in the first person. He addresses Mohammed, and through Mohammed, all mankind.[3] Students of comparative religion have sometimes suggested that one should not
compare the position of the Koran in Islam with the position of the

---

[1] Muh. b. Ismâʾîl a. ʿAbdallâh al-Bukhârî, 810-870 A.D., *GAL* I 157;
Al-Gâmiʿ as-Sahîh, many editions, e.g. *bi-sharh Ahmad b. Muh. al-Qastallânî*,
Cairo (Bûlâq) 1288 A.H., 10 vls.; "Tradition": cf. Lane, *Lexicon*, ii, 529a:
hadîth "new, recent . . . a story . . . a tradition traced up to Mohammad."

[2] *GdQ* I 20-28; W. M. Watt, *Bell's Introduction to the Qurʾân*, 18-25;
On the *hadîth qudsî* cf. *GdQ* I 258-60.

[3] It is not certain whether the Koran, at the time of its revelation, was
supposed to address all mankind or Mohammed's countrymen only. At
present, the Moslems agree that its message is universal.

Bible in Christianity. The Koran, having emanated directly from
God, is, a student of comparative religion might say, the equivalent
of Christ, the Son of God. As Christian theologians have deduced
from Christ's nature his Uncreatedness, so their Moslem colleagues
have inferred from the character of the Koran its Uncreatedness.
In such a scheme of thought, Mohammed, the first person who
brought the message of this uncreated word of God, could be
equated with an Apostle like Paul, the first human being to preach
the significance of Christ's death and resurrection. In an attempt at
explaining the parallelism between the Son of God and the
Book of God, a Canadian scholar wrote: "to look for historical
criticism of the Koran is rather like looking for psychoanalysis
of Jesus."[4]

Although the Uncreatedness of the Koran would seem to preclude
interest in the particulars of its descent into this world, Moslem
theologians have been interested in its historical background. In
the first centuries of Islam they decided for every chapter (*sûra*)
of the Koran for instance whether it had been "sent down" before
or after 622, the year in which the Prophet migrated from Mecca
to Medina. They ascertained for each passage the circumstances
under which it had been revealed, and produced a small but sizable
body of literature on these *asbâb an-nuzûl*, "causes of the revelation".[5] But it should be noted that the Egyptian scholar As-Suyûtî
(1445-1505) remarks in his *Al-Itqân fî ῾Ulûm al-Qur᾽ân* (The
mastery of the sciences of the Koran):[6] "One should not consider
the particular causes, the single unique facts, that brought about
the revelation of a certain chapter or verse; one should rather pay
attention to the general applicability of the wording of the Koran."[7]
In spite of other trends in Koran scholarship, one gets the impression
that with most theologians the interest in the historical particulars
of the revelation process was not very great. For instance, it appears
from the bibliography of books printed in Egypt between 1926 and

---

[4] W. C. Smith, *Islam in Modern History*, Princeton 1957, 17 ff.; In the
Quicumque Athanasianum we read: ... *increatus filius* ...; cf. Schönmetzer,
ed., *Enchiridion Symbolorum*[xxxii], Freiburg 1963, 40; Recently K. Barth,
Kirchliche Dogmatik I, 1, § 11:2: *Der Ewige Sohn* (435 ff.); MacDonald,
Development of Muslim Theology, Lahore 1964, 146-152.

[5] One of the most authoritative works on this subject is Al-Wâhidî,
Asbâb an-Nuzûl, GAL I 411, S I 730.

[6] *GAL* S II 179.

[7] *Al-Itqân*, i, 29: *Hal al-῾ibra bi-῾umûm al-lafz aw bi-khusûs as-sabab.*

1940 that in that period only two titles on *Asbâb an-nuzûl* were printed.[8]

After Mohammed's death in Medina in 632 the Moslem community had many problems to face. Some of these were of a political nature: Who was going to govern the young community? Could the Prophet have a successor? His task of mediating between God and Man, i.e. of transmitting the Koran, had been unique and peculiar to him. Consequently the revelation of the Koran had come to its end at his death. It could never be continued. About this no discussion arose. However, those utterances of Mohammed that were thought to be of divine origin still had to be collected, had to be written down as far as this had not yet been done, and had to be more or less officially edited. These tasks were carried out under the first Caliphs,[9] the deputies of the Prophet in his secular functions.[10]

The script which the Arabs used in those days was not unambiguous, and the imperfect notation of the vowels and the similarity of the shapes of several consonants brought about a long struggle to remove all ambiguities from the written text of the Koran.[11] This process, described by O. Pretzl in the third volume of the *Geschichte des Qorans* found its conclusion in the publication of the printed text of the Koran by an Egyptian Royal Committee of experts in 1924.[12] No other edition ever possessed such general authority.

Reverting to the comparison of Bible with Koran, it should be noted that there is—as opposed to the differences described above—also an important and obvious correspondance: both Bible and Koran are texts from the past, written in languages foreign to many of its readers, languages that have changed and developed since

---

[8] A. I. Nussayr, *Arabic Books 1926-1940*, 23.

[9] "Caliph": from the Arabic *khalîfa*, a noun from the consonantal root *kh-l-f* "to follow, to come after s.o.", hence "to be the successor of s.o."; cf. diadoch, from the Greek διάδοχος, also from a verb meaning "to follow": διαδέχομαι.

[10] *GdQ* II 13-15; 47-50; W. M. Watt, *Bell's Introduction*, 40ff.

[11] The difficulties caused by the similarity in the shapes of the letters were eventually mitigated by adding diacritical points. E.g., ﺏ became ﺏ "b", or ﺕ "t", or ﺙ "th", etc.

[12] *Der Islam*, xx (1932), 2-3; *GdQ* III 273. However, the first printed edition of the Koran is due to European scholarship. It was published in 1834 by Gustav Flügel in Leipzig. On the questions raised by the first redaction and the pre-Uthmanic codices, cf. W. M. Watt, o.c., 44 ff.

the days when these texts were first noted down. Thus most Moslems and Christians need help to interpret, apply and sometimes even translate these texts. Consequently huge libraries of commentaries and (in the case of the Bible) translations have come into existence.

Yet it is not the language problem that has been the historical starting point of the exegesis of Bible or Koran, but the inevitably increasing number of situations not dealt with in the sacred writings. In the case of the Old Testament the need for commentaries arose slowly. There have been periods in which a puzzled believer did not try to find the solution to his new problems in the interpretation of the existing quantity of revelation, but rather hoped for more prophecy in line with earlier revelations to be added to the already existing holy texts. For instance, after the destruction of the Temple in Jerusalem, in 586 B.C., the surviving desperate leaders of Judea asked the prophet Jeremiah for new revelations. They did not try to deduce a course of action from Jeremiah's previous words.[13] In Judaism and Christianity this change of attitude from "hoping for more revelation" to "trying to explain the canonized corpus" took place very gradually.[14] For years there was the possibility that God would send another prophet, for years there was the possibility for a Christian community to receive another authoritative apostolic letter. In the case of Islam, this change of attitude had to take place in a few hours: once Mohammed had died, the source of revelation had definitely dried up. One could not ask him or anyone else for an authoritative apostolic solution to new problems and one could not hope for more revelation to come. It had become imperative to resort to distilling everything out of the extant texts and consequently to resort to an extensive interpretation of them.

The task of supplying the believers with guidance and religious instruction had to be taken over, at short notice, by the theologians, lexicographers, linguists, grammarians and jurists of Islam. We find that the first "professional" among these, Mohammed's nephew Ibn 'Abbâs, was less than fifty years younger than Mohammed himself, and lived as early as 619-670.[15] It is in this light that we

---

[13] Jer. 42.
[14] J. W. Doeve, *Jewish Hermeneutics*, 52 ff.
[15] *EI*[2], i, 40; *GAS* I 25.

should understand the much quoted maxim *Al-'ulamâ' warathat al-anbiyâ'*, "The scholars are the heirs of the Prophets".[16]

The *'Ulamâ'* have taken their task as heirs of the Prophet seriously. They have devoted tremendous efforts to the Koran, but they have not been the only group of Moslems to have worked on it: also calligraphers, bookbinders, printers and reciters have spent their lives excercising their professions in the service of the Koran. Until recently, the only subject of Moslem primary education was the memorization of the Koran. The amount of intellectual energy that has been dedicated to this task by children all over the Moslem world defies the Western imagination.

The work of the Moslem interpreters of the Koran has always attracted the attention of Western observers of Islam. This may surprise the traditional Moslems, since their own interest in the history of the interpretation of the Koran has been limited. Only in the second half of the twentieth century it is no longer exceptional for Moslem scholars to publish books about the history of Koran exegesis.[17] The only important earlier work is As-Suyûtî's *Tabaqât al-Mufassirîn*, (The generations of the interpreters of the Koran), and this book exists only in a Western edition made by the Leiden scholar A. Meursinge in 1839.[18] The Moslem public seems, moreover, traditionally to have been as interested in having the Koran calligraphed or chanted and recited, as in having it interpreted.

The most famous result of Western interest in the history of Koran interpretation is I. Goldziher's *Richtungen der Islamischen Koranauslegung*, translated into Arabic as *Al-Madhâhib al-Islâmiyya fî-t-Tafsîr*.[19] As appears from its title, this book is not a chronology of Moslem Koran interpretation, but an attempt at depicting several trends that may be discerned in the exegesis of the Koran, from the beginning up to Mohammed Abduh (d. 1905). It does not

---

[16] A. J. Wensinck, *Handbook*, 234.

[17] E.g. Mustafâ as-Sâwî al-Guwaynî, *Manhag az-Zamakhsharî*, 1968²; 'Abdallâh Mahmûd Shihâta, *Manhag .. Muhammad 'Abduh ..*, 1959; Muhammad Husayn ad-Dhahabî, *At-Tafsîr wa-l-Mufassirûn*, 1961; 'Abd al-'Azîm Ahmad al-Ghubâshî, *Ta'rîkh at-Tafsîr*, 1971; Abû Yaqzân 'Atiyya al-Gabûrî, *Dirâsât fî Tafsîr wa-Rigâlih*, 1971; 'Iffat Muhammad as-Sharqâwî, *Ittigâhât at-Tafsîr*, 1972.

[18] *De Interpretibus Korani*, Ed. A. Meursinge, Leiden 1839.

[19] Translated by 'Alî Hasan 'Abd al-Qâdir, *Al-Madhâhib al-Islâmiyya fî Tafsîr al-Qur'ân*, Cairo 1944 & reprinted. Cf. L. Gardet & M.-M. Anawati, *Introduction à la théologie musulmane*, 26.

give a periodization of the exegetical literature, and, naturally, leaves out many commentaries—widely studied in the Moslem world—that do not contribute to the aim of the book: the elucidation of the *Richtungen* of Moslem Koran interpretation. In his book I. Goldziher does not mention such commentaries as those of Ibn Kathîr,[20] Al-Âlûsî,[21] An-Nasafî,[22] Abû as-Su'ûd [23] or Abû Hayyân;[24] and the popular commentary by As-Suyûtî and Al-Mahallî, commonly known as *Tafsîr al-Galâlayn*,[25] is mentioned only briefly in a footnote.

I. Goldziher assumes the existence of five *Richtungen*, or tendencies, in the Moslem interpretation of the Koran: (1) the interpretation with the help of Traditions from the Prophet and his contemporaries; (2) dogmatical interpretation; (3) mystical interpretation; (4) sectarian interpretation; (5) modernist interpretation. The weak side of this division becomes apparent when we see that Az-Zamakhsharî, who is of the utmost importance for his philological work on the syntactical analysis of the verses of the Koran, is dealt with in the chapter on dogmatical interpretation because of his being a heterodox theologian, a representative of the Mutazilite school of thought.

In the present study we are mainly concerned with what I. Goldziher might have dealt with in his chapter on modernist interpretation. In order to picture modern Egyptian Koran interpretation, the reader is invited to imagine the Koran exegetes—as has been suggested above—as all working together in a large circular reading room, somewhere in the centre of Cairo. They see the Koran and the exigencies of Koran interpretation from three different viewpoints: natural history, philology and the day-to-day affairs of the Moslems in this world.

Yet all writers present use the same reference library. This reference library contains the Koran commentaries by At-Tabarî (d. 923), Az-Zamakhsharî (d. 1144), Ibn al-Kathîr (d. 1373) and Mohammed Abduh (d. 1905). They quote freely from these books, yet rarely mention them by title. They use the same dictionaries:

---

[20] d. 1373, *GAL* II 49 & S II 48/9.
[21] d. 1854, *GAL* S II 785 ff.
[22] d. 1310, *GAL* II 196 (ix) & S II 267/8 (x).
[23] d. 1574, *GAL* II 438, S II 651.
[24] d. 1344, *GAL* S II 136.
[25] Al-Mahallî, d. 1459 & As-Suyûtî, d. 1505; *GAL* II 114, 145[6] & S II 179[6]-180. Cp. I. Goldziher, *Richtungen*, 346.

those by Ibn Manzûr (d. 1311), Al-Gawharî (d. 1002) and Al-Fîrûzâbâdî (d. 1414). They also use two other books about the Koran: Al-Wâhidî's compilation of the occasions on which specific verses were "sent down" and As-Suyûtî's introduction to the Koran. These books are considered public property: quotations or borrowings from them are rarely acknowledged. They also utilize the same text of the Koran: the text published by the Egyptian Royal Committee of experts in 1924.

Each of them brought along books of his own, e.g. the Koran commentaries by Abû Hayyân, Ar-Râzî, and Abû as-Su'ûd. In our reading room we find additional literature that has seemingly little or nothing to do with the Koran. We find books on natural history, textual criticism and philology as well as general publications on Islam: tracts by leaders of religious organizations, books on Islamic law, collections of sermons, magazines, journals and newspapers. Many of the first-mentioned works are not original, but adaptations of Western books. Although Western influence is great, it seems mainly to come from indirect sources. It is almost impossible to trace back the exact source of the knowledge of Western ideas, and this has caused some observers to think that these sources might sometimes have been oral.

In the room different kinds of activity are going on. The main concern of some exegetes seems to be to prove that the modern sciences are not in contradiction to the Koran, or even that they can be deduced from the Koran. The exegetes who adhere to this view hold that the Koran could only be properly understood after the natural and technical sciences of the nineteenth and twentieth centuries had become known in the Islamic world. Their kind of Koran interpretation is called in Arabic *tafsîr 'ilmî* (scientific exegesis). *Tafsîr 'ilmî* not only has zealous adherents, but also ardent opponents, who argue passionately that it is a "stupid heresy" (*bid'a hamqâ'*).[26] Scientific exegesis will be discussed in the third chapter.

Another group of the Koran interpreters in the reading room considers it their main concern to help their readers to understand the Koran as the contemporaries of the Prophet understood it in the days when the Koran was sent down. According to them, it is not possible to profit from the spiritual guidance the Koran offers

---

[26] Muhammad Kâmil Husayn, *Ad-Dhikr al-Hakîm*, 182.

without first having understood exactly what the Koranic phrases meant. Their work is not unimportant to Western students of the Koran, to whom, moreover, it is bound to be more interesting than other kinds of Koran interpretation. After all, one need not necessarily be a Moslem in order to be interested in the literal meaning of the Koran. Philological exegesis will be discussed in the fourth chapter.

A third group in our reading room has the day-to-day affairs of the Moslems in this world as their main concern. They wonder in how far the Moslems' doings should be influenced by the Koran. They are, sometimes, worried by the influence of the Western world on Islamic spirituality. They cannot agree with the influence in Egypt of Western ideas about justice and social desiderata as far as these ideas come into conflict with the traditional prescripts of Islamic law. They are not sure whether contemporary Egyptian society is "Islamic" enough. According to them, the message of the Koran should be spread through Egyptian society with the help of the religious organizations and their periodicals, through the sermons in the mosque and through the general press. Practical exegesis will be discussed in the fifth chapter.

There seem to be no Koran exegetes who work exclusively on only one of these three aspects of Koran interpretation. The commentaries which they produce are not monopolized by one of the aspects of their work. But there appear to be a few exceptions. Hanafî Ahmad [27] is an exegete who has no real interest in problems other than those raised by Koran interpretation and natural history. Dr. 'Â'isha 'Abd ar-Rahmân Bint as-Shâti'[28] works almost exclusively on Koran interpretation and philology. However, especially the larger commentaries are heterogeneous, and contain, apart from practical exegesis and edifying sermons, philological and "scientific" digressions.

Many of the exegetes are convinced that the Koran is so rich a book that it would be absurd to limit the number of the meanings of its words and verses to one. In consequence of this they sometimes offer a whole list of possible meanings for one rare word, without venturing to decide which is the "real" or "true" one. Although some contemporary Egyptian Koran scholars [29] object

[27] Cf. p. 47.
[28] Cf. p. 68.
[29] Cf. p. 72.

to this unwillingness to commit oneself to only one meaning, it is
not an untraditional practice. For instance, the Koran exegete Al-
Baydâwî (d. 1282) explains the obscure term al-ʿAdiyât (and the
other feminine plural participles) in the beginning of Sura 100 as
referring to angels, stars, souls, horses, or hands of people fighting
for Islam.[30]

The exegetes freely take over each others' ideas. For instance
Dr. Bint as-Shâtiʾ, professor of Arabic at the secular ʿAyn Shams
University, suggests a solution to the problems raised by the oaths
sworn in the beginning of Sura 93: these oaths by the morning and
the evening, two naturally alternating moments of the day, she
assumes to point to the equally natural alternation of periods in
which Mohammed received revelation and periods in which he did
not receive revelation.[31] This idea is taken over by Mahmûd Farag
al-ʿUqda, assistant professor of Arabic at the "clerical" Azhar
University.[32] This is particularly interesting because the Azhar and
the secular universities are two different worlds that have hardly
any contact with each other.

However, it is not only ideas which the Egyptian exegetes take
over from each other. Every now and then it turns out that whole
pages of their works are identical. For instance what Sheikh Higâzî [33] writes about polygamy is identical with the passage on
polygamy printed in the commentary by Muhammad ʿAbd al-
Munʿim Gamâl.[34] However, the latter's commentary mentions the
former' commentary amongst its sources, and contains (acknowledged) quotations from the Koran commentaries by Al-Alûsî, At-
Tabarî and others, so the possibility that it is only accidental that
the name of Higâzî is not mentioned in this particular passage can-

---

[30] It may not be superfluous to mention here that the belief in a plurality
of meanings is also found with Christian theologians. For instance, Thomas
Aquinas teaches that "the differing interpretations must all be true ones,
and . . . they must all agree with the context". Thomas quotes from Augus-
tine: "Etiam secundum litteralem sensum in una littera Scripturae plures
sint sensus." ("Even in the literal sense one passage of Scripture may contain
more than one meaning.") Cf. J. Wilkinson, Interpretation and Community,
186 f., from which these quotations were taken. The problem of ambiguity
in literature, especially in poetry, is not as simple as one would like to think,
as has been demonstrated by W. Empson's Seven Types of Ambiguity.
[31] ʿÂʾisha ʿAbd ar-Rahmân Bint as-Shâtiʾ, At-Tafsîr al-Bayânî[2], i, 17-26.
[32] Mahmûd Farag al-ʿUqda, Tafsîr Guzʾ ʿAmmâ, 98.
[33] Muhammad Mahmûd Higâzî, At-Tafsîr al-Wâdih, iv, 71.
[34] Muhammad ʿAbd al-Munʿim al-Gamâl, At-Tafsîr al-Farîd, 502.

not be ruled out, nor the possibility that both Koran scholars have made use of a common source.

The Egyptian public's interest does not restrict itself to modern commentaries. Commentaries on the Koran which were written before the twentieth century are also still widely read. The so-called *Tafsîr al-Galâlayn*, written in 1466/7, saw at least seven editions between 1926 and 1940 in Cairo,[35] and the Koran commentary by Az-Zamakhsharî, written in 1131/2, was printed at least five times before 1919,[36] and went through no less than three editions between 1926 and 1970 in Cairo.[37] It would be difficult to find an occidental capital where a twelfth century Bible commentary was printed three times within even fifty years, or a fifteenth century one which was printed seven times within fifteen years.[38]

The Egyptian public reads and speaks Arabic. So, naturally, it has no need for translations of the Koran. Yet, especially in the thirties, there have been discussions as to whether it was permissible to translate the Koran. These discussions were intimately connected with the political controversies of the day, especially with Pan-Islamism. The Turkish government, led by Mustafa Kemal Atatürk,[39] had abolished the Caliphate and changed the language of the public call to prayer from Arabic to Turkish. The Turkish rulers also wanted the sermons in the Mosque to be preached in Turkish and not in Arabic, and they favoured the translation of the Koran from Arabic into Turkish. In the five prescribed daily prayers recitation of verses of the Koran is obligatory, and "the question of translating the Koran came to be focused on the issue whether or not the Koran in the Turkish language could be used in these prayers".[40] When the resistance of the Turkish Islamists was overcome by the Atatürk régime, the fight against the translation of the Koran was carried on by the 'Ulamâ' in Egypt.

Rashîd Ridâ took an extreme stand in this controversy. As a "Pan-Islamist" he could not but disapprove of anything that might

---

[35] A. I. Nussayr, *Arabic Books 1926-1940*, nr. 187/2-190/2 & 192/2-193/2, p. 26.

[36] Y. A. Sarkîs, *Mu'gam*, 974-5.

[37] A. I. Nussayr, o.c., 141/2 (sic) & Mustafâ al-Halabî, 4 vls., Cairo 1966.

[38] However, if one would look for biographies of Jesus instead of Bible commentaries and take the eighteenth or nineteenth century instead of the twelfth and the fifteenth century, the results might be different.

[39] 1881-1938, in power since 1922.

[40] N. Berkes, *The Development of Secularism in Turkey*, 487-9.

diminish the unity of the Moslems, such as the abolition of the
Caliphate or the translation of the Koran from the original Arabic
into one of the other languages used by Moslems, languages which
in his eyes served no purpose other than to divide them. According
to Rashîd Ridâ, Arabic was the only true language of the Moslem
world, and he held the opinion that the Turkish government ought
to adopt it as the official language of their country, in order to
prove that the Turks had remained within the realm of Islam.[41]

Once the political fervour of the issue had abated, the translation
debate came to a logical conclusion: the present Egyptian view,
represented e.g. by the late Sheikh Mahmûd Shaltût, holds that
translating the Koran is a way of interpreting it, and that as such
there can exist no obstacles to it. However, the Koran in translation
is not so authoritative as the Koran in its original wording. A
translation of the Koran, as the late Azhar rector Shaltût remarks,
cannot be used as a "root" or "source" of the Islamic doctrine of
duties (fiqh).[42] Given the amount of Christian—sometimes extremely edifying—sermons that are based on clever exploitation of
the accidental phrasing of the Bible translation which happens to
be used by the preacher, sermons that are sometimes quite contrary
to the meaning of the Biblical text in the original language, one
cannot but admire the wisdom behind this Moslem attitude. For
devotional purposes in the prescribed five daily prayers, however,
Shaltût permits the use of a translation of the Koran.

The language of the Koran and (Egyptian) modern standard
Arabic are not fully identical. Certain syntactical constructions,
certain particles, nouns and verbs occur almost exclusively in only
one of these two varieties of Arabic. This difference between contemporary standard Arabic and the seventh century Arabic of the
text of the Koran has given rise to elaborate, translation-like
paraphrases in modern standard Arabic of the text of the Koran.
The largest of these is entitled *Al-Muntakhab fî Tafsîr al-Qur'ân*,
(The better choice in the interpretation of the Koran). It is a
publication of an Egyptian State committee, the "Supreme Council
of Islamic Affairs", *Al-Maglis al-A'lâ li-s-Shu'ûn al-Islâmiyya*.

---

[41] Muhammad Rashîd Ridâ, *Targamat al-Qur'ân wa-mâ fîhâ min Mafâsid
wa-Munâfât al-Islâm*, Cairo 1925/6; Cf. also Muhammad al-Mahyâwî,
Targamat al-Qur'ân al-Karîm 'Arad li-s-Siyâsa wa-Fitna li-d-Dîn, Cairo
1936/7.
[42] Mahmûd Shaltût, *Al-Islâm 'Aqîda wa-Sharî'a*[3], 481.

Portions of this work have appeared as supplements to the periodical edited by the Council, *Minbar al-Islâm*.

Examples from *Al-Muntakhab* are hardly intelligible except in Arabic. For instance, the fourth verse of the first sura of the Koran runs *mâliki-yawmi-d-dîni*. Bell translates this as "Wielder of the Day of Judgment". In this verse one difference between Koranic Arabic and contemporary standard Arabic lies in the use of the last word of the Arabic text, *dîn*. If this word is used at all in modern writing, it means "faith" or "religion", whereas in the Koran its meaning is "religion", "obedience", or "requital". *Al-Muntakhab* now paraphrases this verse as "The King of the Day of Requital and Reckoning", using *gazâ'* "requital" and *hisâb* "reckoning" to paraphrase *dîn*. These two words are both directly and unambiguously understandable in modern standard Arabic.

In the preface to *Al-Muntakhab* the editors inform the reader that they wrote this *tafsîr* "in order to make [the text of the Koran] fit for translation into a foreign language". There is no reason not to call *Al-Muntakhab* a translation of the Koran into modern standard Arabic.

Another kind of Koran commentary brought into existence because of the difference between the language of the Koran and modern standard Arabic, are the school commentaries designated for pupils of secondary schools. The most widely distributed and most often reprinted of these is a commentary in thirty small volumes by three authors, Mahmûd Muhammad Hamza, a former teacher at Dâr al-'Ulûm and inspector of secondary and technical education; Hasan 'Ulwân, a former director of a secondary school; and Muhammad Ahmad Barâniq, an inspector of secondary education.[43]

This commentary is simple: after a passage from the Koran of approximately one page, a list of the Koranic words that are supposed to cause difficulties to secondary school pupils follows. These difficult words are explained in simple modern standard Arabic. After the original Koranic text and the list of difficult words, we again find a translationlike paraphrase of the whole text. This "commentary" may be extremely useful to Western students who have a working knowledge of standard Arabic and who wish to begin their study of the Koran.

---

[43] Published by *Dâr al-Ma'ârif*, Cairo.

Not all Egyptian exegetes working after 1900 tried to write a complete commentary. This is all the more remarkable since all classical commentaries that are still in use are complete, covering word by word the whole text of the Koran, from the first to the last verse. The Arabic term for such a complete uninterrupted commentary is *tafsîr musalsal* or "chained" commentary. At present, about a dozen twentieth century *musalsal* commentaries exist. As far as I can see, they are:

'Abd al-Galîl 'Isâ, *Al-Mushaf al-Muyassar* (± 1961) [44]
'Abd al-Karîm al-Khatîb, *At-Tafsîr al-Qur'ânî li-l-Qur'ân* (± 1967-9)
Ahmad Mustafâ al-Marâghî, *Tafsîr al-Marâghi* (± 1945)
Hâfiz 'Isâ 'Ammâr, *At-Tafsîr al-Hadîth* (± 1959)
Ibn al-Khatîb, *Awdah at-Tafâsîr* (± 1934)
Al-Maglis al-A'lâ li-s-Shu'ûn al-Islâmiyya, *Al-Muntakhab* (1961)
Mahmûd Muhammad Hamza (a.o.), *Tafsîr al-Qur'ân al-Karîm* (1952?)
Muhammad 'Abd al-Mun'im al-Gamâl, *At-Tafsîr al-Farîd* (1952?)
Muhammad 'Abd al-Mun'im Khafâgî, *Tafsîr al-Qur'ân* (1959)
Muhammad Abû Zayd, *Al-Hidâya wa-l-'Irfân* (1930)
Muhammad 'Alî as-Sâyis, *Tafsîr Âyât al-Ahkâm* (1953)
Muhammad Farîd Wagdî, *Al-Mushaf al-Mufassar* (1905)
Muhammad 'Izza Darwaza, *At-Tafsîr al-Hadîth* (1960)
Muhammad Mahmûd Higâzî, *At-Tafsîr al-Wâdih*[2] (1952)
Muhammad Rashîd Ridâ, *Tafsîr al-Manâr* (1901 → 1935)
Mustafâ as-Saqqâ', *Al-Wagîz fî Tafsîr al-Kitâb al-'Azîz* (1967)
Sayyid Qutb, *Fî Zilâl al-Qur'ân* (1950-1960?)

Apart from these giants, innumerable smaller complete commentaries on single suras and on groups of suras exist. Of these, the commentaries by Dr. 'Â'isha 'Abd ar-Rahmân Bint as-Shâti' are probably the most important.[45]

Next to these complete "uninterrupted" commentaries we find "topical" commentaries that treat of specific Koranic subjects, e.g. fasting, divorce, woman, or subjects such as leadership. Scholars working on topical commentaries often stress the fact that the

---

[44] The dates in brackets are the dates of the preface of the first edition, or the approximate dates of first publication. All the books mentioned were printed in Cairo.
[45] Cf. p. 68.

"collection" of the Koran was carried out only after the death of
the Prophet, and that consequently there is little or nothing
"inspired" about the present order of its verses and suras. Times and
intellectual habits having changed, there is nothing against the
establishment of a topically rearranged text of the Koran, a *mushaf
mubawwab*, as Amîn al-Khûlî argues in his *Manâhig Tagdîd* (Programs of renewal).[46]

It is impossible—and unnecessary—to draw a sharp distinction
between "topical" Koran commentaries and books about the Koran
or books about Islam. It would indeed be an unmistakable mark of
"pseudo-scholarship" to attempt to do so. Also the distinction
between complete and topical commentaries is not clear-cut. A
famous intermediate form is the book by the above-mentioned
Sheikh Mahmûd Shaltût, entitled *Tafsîr al-Agzâ' al-'Ashara al-Ûlâ*,
(Commentary on the first ten *agzâ'* of the Koran). (*Agzâ'* is the
plural of *guz'* "a thirtieth part of the Koran". For recitational,
devotional and practical purposes the Koran is divided into thirty
guz'. This division is indicated in most editions of the Koran.)

Shaltût in his *Tafsîr* does not follow the text of the Koran word
by word, but he writes elaborately about the central concepts of
the suras he treats.[47] For instance, in his commentary on Sura 2
he talks at length about the word *birr*, which means according to
Lane's dictionary "piety; kindness; obedience to God; goodness;"
etc. In Sura 2 it occurs more than five times,[48] e.g. in verse (172) 177:

> It is not *virtuous conduct* that ye should turn your faces towards
> the East or the West, but *virtuous conduct* is that of those who
> have believed in Allah and the Last Day, ... who have spoken
> truth, who show *piety*.

For future students of contemporary Islamic thought, Shaltût's
Tafsîr will be an important source but it is not a representative
example of modern Koran interpretation. Before its publication as
a book, this work was printed in the periodical *Risâlat al-Islâm*, a

---

[46] Ahmad as-Sharabâsî, *Qissat at-Tafsîr*, 163; Amîn al-Khûlî, *Manâhig
Tagdîd*, 304-7. In Nagaf (Iraq) a *mushaf mubawwab* appeared in 1969,
compiled by Muhammad Bâqir al-Muwahhid al-Abtahî, who argues that in
Sura 12 the Koran itself systematically arranges the story of Joseph and thus
legitimizes systematical arrangement (*Al-Madkhal ilâ at-Tafsîr al-Mawdû'î*,
Nagaf 1969, p. 8). See also: Muhammad Mahmûd Higâzî, *Al-Wahda al-
Mawdû'iyya fî-l-Qur'ân al-Karîm*, (thesis) Cairo 1970. Cf. further a phrase
like "*Awwal al-Qur'ân fî hâdhâ at-Tartîb* ..." (Abduh, *Tafsîr al-Fatiha*, 17).
[47] Cf. Ahmad as-Sharabâsî, *Qissat at-Tafsîr*, 165 (on Shaltût).
[48] In verse (41)44; (172)177; (185)189; (224)224. Cf. Jer. 7:22-3.

journal devoted to the "unifying of the denominations of Islam",
at-Taqrîb bayn al-madhâhib.[49]

Understandably, Western observers of Islam have been more
interested in Koran commentaries which caused a stir in public
opinion in some way or other, more than in the dozens of commentaries that have not done so. Probably no Bible commentary
which appeared in the Netherlands in the twentieth century ever
reached the front-page of a Dutch newspaper, and neither did most
Koran commentaries that appeared in twentieth century Egypt
attract much attention from Arab journalists. There are, however,
in Egypt a few notable exceptions: the Koran commentaries by
Muhammad Abû Zayd (1930),[50] Ahmad Khalafallâh (1947)[51] and
Mustafâ Mahmûd (1970)[52] did draw wide-spread newspaper attention because of their controversial character. For an outsider it is
difficult, if not impossible, to make a distinction between the
political and theological issues involved in the turmoil created by
these books. The same, of course, holds good for other anathematized
books in which the Koran is obliquely referred to, and which
caused trouble to their authors.[53]

Much has been written by Western observers of Islam about the
commotion concerning these works.[54] But, again, it should be

---

[49] *Risâlat al-Islâm, Magalla Rubʿ Sanawiyya Islâmiyya, Sâhibhâ Muhammad al-Madanî, Dâr at-Taqrîb bayn al-Madhâhib al-Islâmiyya,* Cairo
1949→ ; Shaltût's commentary appears from volume one. Reviews of Shaltût's
commentary: *Magallat al-Azhar,* 32, 112 (June 1960) and 31, 1013 (March
1960).

[50] A. Jeffery, *Der Islam,* xx (1932), 301-8 (on Abû Zayd).

[51] J. Jomier, "Quelques positions actuelles de l'exégèse coranique en
Egypte révélées par une polémique récente (1947-1951)", *MIDEO* 1 (1954),
39-72.

[52] Mustafâ Mahmûd, *Al-Qurʾân, Muhâwala li-Fahm ʿAsrî li-l-Qurʾân,*
Cairo 1970; previously published in the weekly magazine *Sabâh al-Khayr,*
early in 1970; Dr. Bint as-Shâtiʾ's polemics against it, published originally
in the daily newspaper *Al-Ahrâm,* have appeared in book form: *Al-Qurʾân
wa-t-Tafsîr al-ʿAsrî,* Cairo 1970. Several prominent theologians air their
views on Mustafâ Mahmûd's book in the journal of the Moslem Young
Men's Association *Magallat as-Shubbân al-Muslimîn,* e.g. 157 (1-3-1970).

[53] E.g. Tâhâ Husayn, *Fî-s-Shiʿr al-Gâhilî* (1926); or ʿAlî ʿAbd ar-Râziq,
Al-Islâm wa-Usûl al-Hukm (1925). Cp. H. A. R. Gibb, *Modern Trends in
Islam,* 54, and footnotes.

[54] In spite of a sizable amount of publications on Khalafallâh's *Al-Fann
al-Qasasî,* one observation seems not to have been made clearly, viz. that in
this book Khalafallâh seems to have used the exegetical method called
typological by Christian theologians when applied to the Old Testament.
The theory of so-called typological exegesis has its starting point in two

remembered that even during the heights of the agitation about
these "controversial" works, more copies were being printed, sold
and studied of the fifteenth century Galâlayn commentary than of
any of these former works.

---

passages in the Epistles of Paul: "Nevertheless death reigned from Adam
to Moses, even over them that had not sinned after the similitude of Adam's
transgression, who is the figure of him that was to come" (Romans 5:14),
and "All our fathers were under the cloud, and all passed through the sea;
and were all baptized unto Moses in the cloud and in the sea; and did all
drink the same spiritual drink: for they drank of that spiritual rock that
followed them: and that rock was Christ. (. . .) Now these things were our
examples" (1 Corinthians 10:1-6).

The word 'figure' in the passage from the Epistle to the Romans and the
word 'example' at the end of the passage from the Epistle to the Corinthians,
are both translations of the Greek noun *tupoi*, from which the term 'typological exegesis' is derived. In these two passages Paul gives a very special
interpretation of Exodus 13:21 (the "pillar of a cloud" which guided the
Israelites in the desert), of Exodus 17:6 (the rock which Moses smote and
from which the Israelites drank), and to other passages from Exodus, viz.
14:22 and 16:4. (J. Wilkinson, *Interpretation and Community*, 95 ff.).

Roman Catholic theologians like H. de Lubac and J. Daniélou have
elaborated these interpretations by Paul into a system that they consider
to be applicable to the whole of the Old Testament. (H. H. Miskotte, *Sensus
Spiritualis*, 123-137). However, by reducing the 'pillar' and the 'rock' to
'shadows of things to come', an exegete goes against the intention of the
human compilers of the text of the Old Testament and against the intentions
of those who canonized these texts. Also, the public to which these texts
were primarily addressed, did not think of things to come: to them these
texts and the stories told in them had a value of their own.

When, on the other hand, the Koran talks about the Prophets before
Mohammed, the stories as told by the Koran always foreshadow Mohammed
and have little to do with the history of the Prophet they seem to tell about.
(Cf. A. Jeffery, *The Koran as Scripture*). For instance, the Koran tells how
people "put their fingers in their ears" when hearing Noah preach; the first
hearers of the Koran will have thought of how Mohammed was ridiculed by
his fellow-Meccans when they listened to Noah's story as told in Koran
71:(5)5 - (6)7. When they listened to the Koranic version of a prayer
said by Noah (Koran 71:(27) 26 - (29) 28): "Oh Lord, leave not upon the
earth of the unbelievers a household . . . their every birth will be a scamp
unbelieving . . . O my Lord, pardon me and my parents", they cannot have
failed to realize that Mohammed's own parents had died as pagans before
the advent of Islam.

Khalafallâh, in his *Al-Fann al-Qasasî*, hints at the typological method
of interpreting the Koranic scripture when, for instance, he writes: "The
picture the Koran gives of the Prophets Hûd and Shu'ayb and of how
they debated with their fellow-tribesmen, is a general picture which applies
to every Prophet. It applies to the Arab Prophet Mohammed" (p. 278);
and: "If we try to understand the spiritual excitement of Abraham and
Moses [when they destroyed the idols of their fellow-tribesmen] we inevitably
understand the circumstances under which Mohammed preached" (p. 280).

Modern Egyptian Koran interpretation [55] is still largely traditional. This is demonstrated not only by the interest which the
general public take in the "classical" commentaries, but also by
the "traditional" contents of many "modern" commentaries. Newness and originality are exceptional; adaptations and moderniza-
tions of the contents of especially Az-Zamakhsharî are the rule.
Often a passage in a modern commentary is hard to understand
unless one has first consulted Az-Zamakhsharî or Galâlayn. Modern
Egyptian commentaries are thus still part or the great tradition of
classical *tafsîr*, as their voluminousness already suggests: it would
not be easy to fill thirty volumes of more than two hundred pages
each with original ideas about a text that has been studied for
more than a thousand years. The only real innovations were introduced by Mohammed Abduh (d. 1905) and Amîn al-Khûlî (d. 1967).

---

[55] The most important new Koran commentaries in the Arab world
outside Egypt are: (1) ʿAbd al-Qâdir al-Maghrabî, *Tafsîr Guzʾ Tabâraka*
(1919, in the style of Abduh's *Tafsîr Guzʾ ʿAmmâ*); Syria; (2) Muhammad
ʿIzza Darwaza (Darûza ?), *At-Tafsîr al-Hadîth*, a Koran commentary in
which the suras are chronologically rearranged, a novelty for the Moslem
world; Palestine; and (3) Muhammad at-Tâhir ibn ʿÂshûr, *Tafsîr at-Tahrîr
wa-t-Tanwîr*; Tunis.

CHAPTER TWO

MOHAMMED ABDUH'S KORAN INTERPRETATION

Before Abduh [1] the interpretation of the Koran was mainly an academic affair. Commentaries were written by scholars for other scholars. Understanding a commentary required detailed knowledge of the technicalities and terminology of Arabic grammar, Moslem law and dogmatics, the Traditions of the Prophet Mohammed and his contemporaries, and the Prophet's biography.[2] The commentaries on the Koran had become encyclopaedias of these sciences, or rather excerpts of encyclopaedias. It took an enormous

---

[1] Mohammed Abduh was born a short time before 1850 in the Egyptian countryside. His exact birthplace and date of birth are not known. In 1862 he began to study at the Ahmadî mosque in Tantâ. After a spiritual crisis in 1865 he became interested in mysticism. His uncle Shaykh Darwîsh introduced him to the Shâdhilî-order. Young Abduh became an ardent Sufi, and in 1866 he took up his studies at the Azhar University in Cairo. In 1869 he met a certain Gamâl ad-Dîn, known as Al-Afghânî, and was strongly influenced by the theories of this political agitator and theologian. Al-Afghânî was originally a Persian Shi'ite, educated in a *madhhab* which still allowed and practised *Igtihâd* (though in Al-Afghânî's *madhhab* this term did not have the same meaning as in Sunni Islam). (N. R. Keddie, *Sayyid Jamâl ad-Dîn "al-Afghânî", A Political Biography*, 1972, 10-37). Al-Afghânî's influence may be responsible for Abduh's later emphasis on the urgency of re-opening the *"gate of Igtihâd"*.

In 1877 Abduh completed his studies at the Azhar University. Between 1877 and 1882 he worked as a journalist and teacher. For his participation, or at least involvement, in the 'Urâbî revolt in 1882 he was condemned to exile. The days of his exile were spent in Beirut, Syria, Paris and elsewhere. In 1888 he was pardoned, returned to Egypt, and was appointed judge, by the then Khedive Tawfîq Pâshâ. When in 1892 'Abbâs Hilmî became Khedive, Abduh suggested to him reforms of the Azhar University, which were partly carried out. As C. C. Adams pointed out (*Islam and Modernism in Egypt*, 72), Abduh was never appointed Rector of the Azhar, although I. Goldziher (*Richtungen*, 321) seems to suppose so.

In 1899 Abduh was appointed *Muftî* of Egypt. Also he became appointed member of the Legislative Council. He died in Alexandria in July 1905. (C. C. Adams, *Islam and Modernism in Egypt*, 1933, "Muhammad 'Abduh: Biography", Chapter II-IV, 18-103).

[2] Abduh writes, e.g.: *"Hâdhâ lâ yanbaghî an yusammâ tafsîr wa-innamâ huwa darb min at-tamrîn fî-l-funûn ka-n-nahw wa-l-ma'ânî wa-ghayrhimâ"*, *Tafsîr al-Manâr*, i, 24; and: *"At-tafsîr ... 'ibâra 'an al-ittilâ' 'alâ mâ qâlhu ba'd al-'ulamâ' fî kutub at-tafsîr"*, o.c. i, 25. Amîn al-Khûlî summarizes Abduh's views as follows: *"Wa-l-ahamm fî-t-tafsîr an yakûn muhaqqiq li-hidâyat al-Qur'ân"*, and *"Al-maqsad al-haqîqî al-ihtidâ' bi-l-Qur'ân"*, *Manâhig Tagdîd*, 302.

amount of intellectual energy to profit from the knowledge stored up in the existing commentaries, which treated anything but the "plain" and "literal" meaning of the Koran. To this kind of scholarly exegesis Abduh objected on principle.

To quote Abduh: "On the Last Day God will not question us on the opinions of the commentators and on how they understood the Koran, but he will question us on his Book which he sent down to guide and instruct us".[3] Abduh intended to explain the Koran in a practical manner to a public wider than merely the professional theologians, an Egyptian public that—according to the modern Moslem apologists—lacked competent religious leaders, suffered from foreign (British) occupation, did not understand the technical sciences and among whom superstition had become predominant. Abduh tries to make his readers, laymen and theologians alike, realize the limited relevance of the traditional commentaries that do not contribute to the solution of the urgent problems of the day.[4] He wishes to convince them that they should allow the Koran to speak for itself, unobscured [5] by subtle explanations and glosses.

Abduh's Koran commentaries [6] and their continuations by Rashîd Ridâ did not have immediate succes.[7] In 1905, more than four years after Abduh's lectures that were to become the Manar commentary had started, Farîd Wagdî complains in the introduction to his own Koran commentary that no commentary existed that was suitable for the layman, devoid of superfluous technicalities and relevant to the turbulent times Egypt was going through.[8] Al-Manfalûtî ridicules Abduh (and Qâsim Amîn [9]) in an

---

[3] *Tafsîr al-Manâr*, i, 26.

[4] o.c., i, 12: *hâgat al-ʿasr*.

[5] o.c., i, 10: *higâb ʿalâ al-Qurʾân*.

[6] Abduh's exegetical work consists of: *Tafsîr al-Manâr*, 1900/01 and later; *Tafsîr Sûrat al-ʿAsr*, 1903; *Tafsîr Guzʾ ʿAmmâ*, 1904; Cf. *GAL* S III 320. Abduh's *Tafsîr Sûrat al-Fâtiha* (1905), which contains an important general introduction to Koran exegesis, has also been printed, with enlargements by Rashîd Ridâ, in the beginning of the first volume of *Tafsîr al-Manâr* (1927). Cf. also C. C. Adams, *Islam and Modernism . . .*, 199.

[7] This is admitted by Abduh himself: "*Yûgad min ashâbî man yaʿtaqid anna tark hâdhâ ad-dars khayr lî min qirâʾatih . . . wa-innahû muthîr li-hasad al-hâsidîn lî . . .*" (*Tafsîr al-Manâr*, iv, 23). Cp. also Anwar al-Gundî, *Tarâgim al-Aʿlâm al-Muʿâsirîn*, 423: "*Lam taʿrifhû Misr . . .*"

[8] Muhammad Farîd Wagdî, *Al-Mushaf al-Mufassar*, preface. (Ed. *Kitâb as-Shaʿb*, n.d., Cairo).

[9] 1865-1908; an advocate of a certain degree of emancipation of the Egyptian women. (*GAL* S III 330).

article originally published in the Moslem newspaper *Al-Mu'ayyad*,[10] and this, as the context of the article indicates, some time after Abduh's death.

Eventually, however, Abduh's commentaries became very successful. They are much quoted by later commentators. At present they are hold to be authoritative by both progressive and conservative Egyptian Moslem theologians. This success may be ascribed to the interest in them by the gradually rising class of Egyptians that had received an education outside the traditional religious institutions. Literacy had, previously, been limited to Egyptians who had received religious training and who consequently were able to use and understand the traditional commentaries in their original form. After the turn of the century, for the first time in the history of Moslem Egypt, considerable numbers of people had learned to read and write outside the mosque. Increasing numbers of Egyptians were coming into contact with Western non-Islamic culture and began to ask questions for which the traditional commentaries had no answer. Abduh's commentaries appealed to the same groups of literates that established, in 1907, political parties which advocated the granting of a constitution (*dustûr*) to Egypt and withdrawal of the British.[11]

In spite of occasional attempts to characterize Abduh as an agnostic,[12] Abduh's religious attitude would be best described as "rationalist". This is also demonstrable from his Koran commentaries. A short sura like Sura 80, which occupies less than two pages in the Egyptian Royal Edition of the Koran, will provide

---

[10] The articles by Mustafâ Luftî al-Manfalûtî have been collected in his *An-Nazarât* (several editions). The article on Abduh and Qâsim Amîn appears on p. 106 of the 1910 edition. Abduh and Qâsim Amîn are mentioned on page 112. Al-Manfalûtî's articles appeared mainly in *Al-Mu'ayyad*, the newspaper which had also published the articles on feminism by Qâsim Amîn that were to be collected in his *Tahrîr al-Mar'a* (1899).

[11] In 1907 three political parties were founded in Egypt. The "literate" character of these organizations may be inferred from the fact that they were centred around newspapers: The *Hizb al-Umma* around *Al-Jarîda*; ʿAli Yûsuf's *Hizb al-Islâh* around *al-Mu'ayyad*; Mustafâ Kâmil's *Al-Hizb al-Watanî* around *Al-Liwâ*. These parties seem to have been more committees of activists than political parties in the present sense of the word. Their programs were, for instance, silent on the gravest problem of Egypt at the turn of the century: the conditions of the peasants, the *fallâhîn*.

[12] Cf. my " "I suspect that my friend Abdu (...) was in reality an Agnostic" " in P. W. Pestman, ed., *Acta Orientalia Neerlandica*, Leiden 1971, p. 71.

some examples of this *rationalisme religieux* which L. Gardet and
M.-M. Anawati call Abduh's *attitude de base*.[13]

The first verses of Sura 80 run:

> He frowned and turned away,
> because the blind man came to him.
> What will he let thee know?
> Mayhap he will purify himself,
> or let himself be reminded,
> and the reminder profit him.[14]

The classical commentaries, as well as Abduh, explain that during
a discussion of Mohammed with some Meccan notables a blind man,
a distant relative of Mohammed's wife Khadîga, came up to Mohammed, who took no notice of him but "frowned and turned
away", continuing his attempts at converting the local dignitaries,
who were not blind but, perhaps, visionless. Abduh then adds that
these verses prove that the message of Islam should be brought to
everyone with a clear intellect [15] regardless of his social position.

Verses 8 and 9 of this sura read: "As for him who comes eagerly,
being in fear, him dost thou neglect".[16] The classical commentaries
explain that the blind man was in fear because of his sins, or because of repercussions that might result from his contact with
Mohammed, who at that time was on bad terms with the local *élite*,
or because though blind he had no guide.

Abduh on the contrary mentions neither sin nor repercussions nor
guide, but explains that the blind man's problem was his thirst for
knowledge: he was afraid he would not be able to purify himself
from his ignorance, would never be illumined by the light of knowledge, and would be left in the darkness of error. Another illustration of Abduh's rather intellectualist concept of fear is to be found
in his comment on Koran 79:26(26): "Surely in that is a lesson for
those who fear". Abduh here teaches that "those who fear" can be
paraphrased as "those who have the intellect to reflect".

The high importance Abduh attached to the human intellect is
also apparent from his treatment of the term *Furqân* [17] which
occurs in Koran 3:4(3):

---

[13] L. Gardet & M.-M. Anawati, *Introduction à la théologie musulmane*.
[14] Bell's translation.
[15] *ᶜaql dhakî*.
[16] Bell's translation.
[17] On the original meaning of the Koranic *Furqân*, cf. R. Paret, "Furkân"
in *EI²* and W. M. Watt, *Bell's Introduction to the Qurʾân*, 145-7.

There is no god but He, the Living, the Eternal; He hath sent
down to thee the Book with truth, confirming what was before
it and He sent down the Torah and the Evangel aforetime as guidance for the people, and He sent down the Furqan.[18]

The word *Furqân*, which is connected with a root F-R-Q meaning
"to discriminate", is left untranslated by Bell. The Dutch Koran
translator J. H. Kramers renders the word as *de onderscheiding*.[19]
The older commentaries explain the word as "anything that makes
a separation or distinction between truth and falsity" or "Book of
Law revealed to Moses in which a distinction is made between that
which is allowable and that which is forbidden." The Galâlayn
commentary explains: "The word is mentioned after Torah,
Evangel and Koran as a general expression covering the books of
revelation not enumerated in these verses". Az-Zamakhsharî
writes: "If you would ask me what is meant by *al-Furqân* I say: the
category of heavenly books because they discriminate between
truth and falsity". Al-Baydâwî informs us: "It is as if the text of
the Koran should be read as follows: He sent down Torah and
Evangel as guidance for the people and He sent down all other
revelations". Ar-Râzî's explanation of *Furqân* comes close to the
Biblical "knowledge of good and evil", and also At-Tabarî connects
Furqân and ethics. Thus, the classical commentaries do not agree
as to whether *Furqân* means 'Holy books' in general or whether it
refers to one particular Holy book, but they do agree on two points:
thanks to that which is designated as *Furqân* we distinguish between
right and wrong, and *Furqân* is not of this world but is transcendent.
Furqân is definitely something revealed.

Abduh treats of this word in an untraditional way. In the Manar
commentary (noted down by Rashîd Ridâ after Abduh's lectures)
we read: "Our Teacher and Leader [i.e. Mohammed Abduh] said
that *Furqân* is reason, by which man discern between truth and
falsity". This statement does not seem remarkable if one has not
consulted the classical commentaries but if one has, it does certainly look suggestive if not provocative: Abduh seems to have
replaced revelation by reason. An implication of this view of Abduh
seems to be that if one wishes to know why he should not kill, or

---

[18] Bell's translation.
[19] J. H. Kramers, *De Koran uit het Arabisch vertaald*, Amsterdam 1956.
Dictionaries render *onderscheiding* as "distinction".

not ask interest on capital, it is sufficient for him to use his intellect, and he does not need to consult Scripture.[20]

Many Egyptians have acclaimed Abduh's Koran commentaries as new and original,[21] which they certainly were. This newness, however, is not one of form. In 1903 Abduh published a commentary on the last 30th part of the Koran, *Guz' 'Ammâ*. In its first edition it contains 190 pages. The suras and verses are not numbered, which is in accordance with traditional usage. The text of the Koran is printed at the top of the page, taking up not more than four lines, the rest of the page is taken up by the commentary, which is printed in smaller type. In the commentary the text of the Koran is repeated, and each word or phrase from the Koran (placed in brackets) is followed by its explanation. Every sura has a brief general introduction, and sometimes there are short digressions on general subjects. The book looks more like a commentary on the words of the Koran than on its verses, pericopes or suras. Its appearance thus does not strike the reader who is acquainted with commentaries such as those by An-Nasafî or Az-Zamakhsharî as new.

The so-called Manar commentary differs in some respects from Abduh's first commentary. Abduh gave a series of lectures on the Koran at the Azhar university, and his Syrian pupil

---

[20] Later Egyptian commentators do not always follow Abduh in this abrupt change from a transcendent view of *Furqân* to an immanent one. Muhammad Abû Zayd is vaguer than Abduh and defines *Furqân* as the ability to distinguish between truth and error. The possession of this ability is not necessarily limited to Moslems. Darwaza and Sayyid Qutb think that *Furqân* is an epithet of *Qur'ân*, a possibility mentioned in the classical commentaries. Several modern Turkish Koran translations render the text of the Koran in accordance with this view. Amîn al-Khûlî in his Koran dictionary (cf. p. 61) gives three meanings (argument, victory, a name of the revealed book) and thus does not follow Abduh. Ahmad Mustafâ al-Marâghî seems the only Egyptian commentator who accepts Abduh's rationalist interpretation of *Furqân*.

Abduh's views on the relationship of reason and revelation are discussed in 'Abdallâh Mahmûd Shihâta's *Manhag al-Imâm Muhammad 'Abduh fî Tafsîr al-Qur'ân al-Karîm*, Cairo 1963, p. 83: "*Inna al-wahy masdar hidâya, wa-l-'aql al-insânî masdar hidâya, wa-kilâhumâ yahduf ilâ tahdîd at-tarîq al-mustaqîm fî hayât al-insân wa-ilâ tahdîd ghâyatih fî hâdhâ al-wugûd . . . lâ budd an yatawâfaqâ . . . (etc.)*".

[21] E.g. Shihâta, o.c., p. *M*; Muhammad Husayn ad-Dhahabî, *At-Tafsîr wa-l-Mufassirûn*, iii, 214; Muhsin 'Abd al-Hamîd, *Al-Âlûsî Mufassiran*, Baghdad 1968, 4; 'Abbâs Mahmûd al-'Aqqâd, "Tafsîr al-Ustâdh al-Imâm" in *Magallat al-Azhar*, xxxv, 389b (November 1963).

Rashîd Ridâ attended these lectures and took notes, which he afterwards revised and enlarged. The result was shown to Muhammad Abduh who approved, or corrected as necessary. These lectures began to appear in [the periodical] *Al-Manâr*, volume iii (A.D. 1900), as the commentary of Muhammad Abduh; since the editor thought it proper, so long as Abduh had read what had been written, to ascribe them to him. The commentary that resulted from this cooperation is known as the Manâr commentary.

It was continued by Rashîd Ridâ alone, after the death of Mohammed Abduh, from Sura 4:125 to Sura 12:107.[22] Ridâ faithfully indicated, in those parts for which he and Abduh were jointly responsible, where the Master's words ended and where his own enlargements began.

The Manar commentary treats of the whole text of the first twelve thirtieth of the Koran, in twelve volumes, each covering one thirtieth part of the Koran. Every volume contains approximately 500 pages. Departing from traditional practice, suras and verses are numbered. The verses are grouped together in logical unities, pericopes of five to ten verses, followed by several pages of commentary. The commentary, which treats of the whole text of the passages under consideration, is frequently interrupted by long digressions in which general problems of religion and society are discussed. Each volume is preceded by indexes in which one finds in alphabetical order the topics which have been touched upon. These alphabetical indexes, a novelty introduced by the Manar commentary, have been imitated by many later Egyptian Koran commentators. The outward appearance of the Manar commentary reminds one of the Koran commentary by Ibn Kathîr,[23] who also divides the text into pericopes.

The newness of Abduh's Koran commentaries springs from the fresh emphasis Abduh puts on the Koran as a source of *hidâya*, religious and spiritual guidance.[24] In Abduh's view the Koran is not

---

[22] C. C. Adams, *Islam and Modernism in Egypt*, 199. This account is based on Rashîd Ridâ's introduction to the first volume of *Tafsîr al-Manâr* which was for the first time published in its present form in 1927. Cf. Adams, o.c., 273.

[23] On Ibn Kathîr's influence on Rashîd Ridâ: cf. Shihâta, o.c., 214. According to A. I. Nussayr, Ibn Kathîr's Koran commentary was printed in 1929 (Matbaʿat al-Manâr) and 1937, which indicates a certain degree of popularity. (A. I. Nussayr, o.c., 170/2 & 171/2).

[24] *Tafsîr al-Manâr*, i, 17: "*Wa-t-tafsîr alladhî natlubuh huwa fahm al-Kitâb min haythu huwa dîn yurshid an-nâs ilâ mâ fîhî saʿâdathum fî hayâthim*

primarily the source of Islamic law or dogmatics, or an occasion for philologists to display their ingenuity, but it is the book from which Moslems ought to derive their ideas about this world and the world to come. From this follow Abduh's different ideas about the exigencies of Koran interpretation. The nucleus of Abduh's exegetical system—if the word "system" may properly be used in this respect—is his hesitation in accepting material from outside the Koran itself as meaningful towards its interpretation.

An exegetical rule which, consequently, lies behind all his exegetical work and is repeated throughout his commentaries in different words, is that one should not explain things that are left unexplained, *mubham*, by the Koran.[25] (The word *mubham*, translated in Lane's dictionary as "closed" or "locked, so that one cannot find the way to open it" came to mean, in modern standard Arabic, "obscure, dark, cryptic, doubtful, vague, ambiguous"—Wehr's dictionary—when applied to words.) An example from Sura 2:(55) 58 may serve to illustrate the meaning of this. In this verse, God speaks to the Jews during their conquest of the promised land (cp. the contents of the book of Joshua): "Enter this town and eat comfortably from it wherever ye please; enter the gate doing obeisance."[26]

The context does not indicate which town the Koran here refers to. Sayyid Qutb and Ahmad Mustafâ al-Marâghî suppose that Jerusalem is meant; Az-Zamakhsharî, Al-Baydâwî, Ibn Kathîr and Farîd Wagdî think it is Jerusalem or Jericho. Abduh then differs radically from both the ancient and the modern commentators and writes: "We shall not try to determine which town is meant in this verse, since the Koran did not try to determine this either. The importance of the verse does not depend upon the exact determination of such particulars"—but lies in the admonition to thankfulness towards God.[27] The word "town" in Sura 2: (55)58 can be explained by a synonym if the Koran used a word that is not directly and unambiguously understandable in modern standard Arabic, but further interpretation is impossible: the word is "closed" to further identification—for which there is no need in any case.

---

ad-dunyâ wa-hayâthim al-âkhira"; and o.c., i, 25: "Fa-l-maqsad al-haqîqî warâ [funûn wa-shurût at-tafsîr] huwa al-ihtidâ᾽ bi-l-Qur᾽ân".

[25] Shihâta, o.c., 137, "manhag al-Imâm fî-l-mubham"; Ad-Dhahabî, o.c., iii, 226: "mawqifuh min mubhamât al-Qur᾽ân".

[26] Tafsîr al-Manâr, i, 323 and i, 344.

[27] Tafsîr al-Manâr, i, 324.

"If God had considered more details in the text of the Koran to be useful, he would have added them."[28]

An exegete is thus obliged to explain the text as it stands and not to supply, for instance, the proper names of the persons and places left anonymous by the Koran. An exegete has no right, is in fact forbidden, to identify anything that is left unidentified by the Koran itself.

In order to determine the meaning of a certain verse or word, Abduh makes ample use of its context. This may seem a pedestrian thing to do, but many exegetes before—and after—Abduh confined themselves, when trying to find out what a certain passage meant, to the traditional explanations as given by At-Tabarî, Ar-Râzî, Az-Zamakhsharî and others, attempting to make a sensible choice out of the masses of material these commentaries offer.[29]

Abduh often succeeds in solving problems by considering the context of a problematical phrase.[30] For instance, in Koran 3:(32) 37 we read:

> Whenever Zechariah entered the sanctuary to see her, he found beside her provisions.
> Said he: "Oh Mary, how hast thou this?"
> She replied: "It is from Allah; Allah provides for whom he willeth".[31]

Al-Baydâwî and Az-Zamakhsharî state that these "provisions" were "the fruits of summer during winter" or "the fruits of the winter season during the summer". This explanation can still be found in a commentary written by the Egyptian judge Hâfiz 'Isâ 'Ammâr in 1960. Sayyid Qutb, in his commentary on this verse, also alludes to the "numerous stories" connected with the indeed miraculous nature of these divine provisions.

Abduh, however, points out that the end of this passage, "Allah provides *for whom* he willeth", shows that the mere presence of the provisions presents the miracle, and not their nature. If their nature had been miraculous, Abduh seems to imply, the end of the passage would have run: "Allah provides *with what* he willeth". Abduh continues his commentary on these verses by saying that taking notice of the context relieves the Moslems of the obligation

---

[28] *Tafsîr Guz' 'Ammâ*, 59.

[29] *Tafsir al-Manâr*, i, 19: "*yumkin an yaqûl ba'd ahl hâdhâ al-'asr: lâ hâga ilâ at-tafsîr ... li-anna al-a'imma as-sâbiqîn nazarû fî-l-kitâb ... fa-mâ 'alaynâ illâ an nanzur fî kutubhim wa-nastaghniy bihâ*".

[30] Shihâta, o.c., 35/9: "*I'tibâr as-Sûra wahda mutanâsiqa*".

[31] Bell's translation.

to believe in a miracle that has been worked by the exegetes. "The Koran explains itself to everybody; there is no need to go into the defence of miracles that are contrary to the plain meaning (*zâhir*) of the words of the Koran."[32]

Abduh denies the authority and the validity of certain traditions handed down from the first generations of Moslems.[33] He does not recognize their relevance to the interpretation of the Koran, even though the exegetes of the past have used these traditions extensively. This applies especially to the so-called *Isrâ'îliyyât* traditions,[34] of which Abduh's pupil Rashîd Ridâ even maintained that they had been fabricated for the purpose of undermining Islam.[35] Abduh goes further in this respect than most of his contemporaries and even claims the right to reject any tradition that does not conform to his understanding of Islam and the Koran, whether a Tradition is one of the *Isrâ'îliyyât* or not, one should not, according to Abduh, "add" to the text of the Koran.[36]

Often Abduh uses all three arguments together, as for instance in the beginning of Sura 89 (where the word *fagr* "daybreak" elicited exegetical speculations): the classical interpretations are rejected because they try to explain something left unexplained by the Koran, do not take into consideration the context and base themselves on a tradition that is suspect—though in this case the "suspect" tradition is ascribed to Mohammed's nephew Ibn 'Abbâs.[37]

---

[32] Shihâta, o.c., 38; *Tafsîr al-Manâr*, iii, 293.

[33] Ad-Dhahabî, o.c., iii, 239: "*Inkâruh li-ba'd al-ahâdîth as-sahîha*".

[34] The Koran, in relating a story, pays more attention to the message and to the religious values of the events related than to the events themselves. Sometimes the story itself is hardly recorded in spite of the importance the Koran attaches to the religious lessons that can be drawn from it. In this way the text of the Koran evokes many questions as to the details and background of certain narratives. The first generations of Moslems tried to answer these questions. In the case of stories that were recorded both in the Bible and the Koran, they frequently did so by consulting Jewish and Christian converts to Islam. The sometimes biblical, sometimes pseudo-biblical material which thus entered Islam, and the Koran commentaries, are known as *Isrâ'îliyyât*. Modernist Moslems often reject the *Isrâ'îliyyât* traditions because of their irrational, miraculous and fantastical character. Abduh writes, in his *Tafsîr al-Fâtiha*, p. 6: "*lâ yutâbiq al-'aql ...*" "it is not commensurate with Reason".

[35] Cf. Ad-Dhahabî, o.c., iii, 254: Rashîd Ridâ even attempted to refute some *Isrâ'îliyyât* traditions with the help of original Biblical material; *Tafsîr al-Manâr*, vi, 330 ff.

[36] *Tafsîr al-Manâr*, i, 347; iv, 268; etc.

[37] Ibn 'Abbâs' reliability is subject to attack e.g. from I. Goldziher, *Richtungen*, 65-81.

Abduh considers the text of the Koran to be generally applicable (*ʿâmm*).[38] An illustration of what this means may be found in his commentary on Sura 92:(14)14-(17)17:

> So I warn you of a fire that blazes
> In which shall roast only the most miserable
> Avoid it shall the most pious [39]

According to the classical commentaries, the "most pious" referred to in this verse is Mohammed's father-in-law, one of the first converts to Islam,[40] Abû Bakr, who became Caliph after the death of Mohammed, from 632-634. The "most miserable" is identified as Abû Gahl or Umayya ibn Khalaf, both well-known enemies of the Prophet.[41] These identifications may be correct, and they may not. The Koran naturally alludes frequently to contemporary events, and such allusions may or may not have been recognized by the first generations of Koran scholars.

Abduh, however, departing from the traditional practice, does not, in the almost eight pages devoted to these verses, mention Abû Bakr, Abû Gahl or Umayya ibn Khalaf, but exhorts, admonishes and warns his contemporaries, pious and impious alike. He con-

---

[38] As in all scriptural religions it is a recurring point of discussion in Islam whether the Holy Scripture is "general" (Ar. *ʿâmm*) or "specific" (Ar. *khâss*). If a text is *khâss* it was revealed with regard to one particular occasion and does not have universal validity. The simplest example of a text that is undoubtedly *khâss* is the command to Moses "Go to Pharao", since this command did not concern anyone but Moses. It was not addressed to all mankind. If a text is *khâss*, specific, the exegetes try to deduce the general rule behind the text, (Ar. *taʿmîm*, "to make general") and to find out how such a general rule can in turn be made applicable to other situations (Ar. *takhsîs*, "to make specific"). If, on the other hand, a text is *ʿâmm*, general, like the Biblical command "Love thy neighbour", it would be wrong to think that this command only addressed a certain pharisee who happened to be in discussion with Jesus. Such a general command addresses other people as well. Thus, Moslem doctrine holds the commands of the Jewish and Christian scriptures to be *khâss*, viz. addressed to Jews and Christians only, and hence of no importance to others. Many Moslem theologians regard the Koran as *khâss* unless the text itself contains indications that it is *ʿâmm*. The Andalusian theologian Ibn Hazm (d. 1064), however, considers a text to be *ʿâmm*, if there is no proof of the contrary in the text itself. These problems are discussed in the sometimes rather hair-splitting works on the so-called *Usûl al-Fiqh*. If a text is *khâss* this has the advantage that there are many ways of constructing the *ʿilla*, "principle", behind such a text. Cf. e.g. I. Goldziher, *Die Zâhiriten*, 120 ff.

[39] Bell's translation.

[40] W. M. Watt, *Muhammad at Mecca*, 86.

[41] ib., e.g. 123.

cludes his edifying sermon with a small paragraph pointing out
that by interpreting these verses in his way, the problems of iden-
tifying the "most pious" and the "most miserable" are solved;
nothing prevents us from believing that also Abû Bakr is referred
to, so he says, but the meaning of these verses of the Koran is
general, "as you have seen." (*Ma'nâ al-âyât lâ yazâl 'âmm kamâ
ra'ayta, w-Allâhu a'lam.*) [42]

Abduh was never a theorist. He was an activist who advocated
immediate practical reform. He had a program for the reform of
Moslem higher education and for the reform of the administration
of Moslem law, but he lacked a consistent overall theory. This also
holds good for his activities in the field of Koran exegesis. He
reluctantly embarked upon it, we are told, under pressure of his
friend, pupil and collaborator Rashîd Ridâ, who was too much of
a professional theologian to permit their programs of reform to go
without a solid Koranic foundation. It was Rashîd Ridâ also who
took upon himself the task to note down Abduh's commentary,
but while doing so he added traditions and grammatical analysis,
be it with the sole purpose of supporting Abduh's views. For instance, in the explanation of the word *Furqân*,[43] Ridâ adds that
Furqân is an infinitive from its root *F-R-Q* in the same way in
which *Qur'ân* "Koran" is an infinitive from its root *Q-R-'*, and
Ghufrân "forgiveness" from its root *GH-F-R*. He probably says so
because an infinitive of this type [44] is comparatively rare. Although
this kind of enlargement is "no doubt beneficial", as Muhammad
Abû Zuhra puts it,[45] it is certainly not something which Mohammed
Abduh would have done himself. Abduh was reluctant to start
another Koran commentary and thus add to the enormous library
of exegetical literature, precisely because Koran exegesis had come
to mean, for the Moslems of his time, cataloguing such rather
pedantic pieces of erudition. He wanted his commentary to be an
instrument by which Moslems could help themselves to be guided
spiritually by means of the Koran itself. So he wanted Koran
commentaries to be without theoretical speculations, grammatical

---

[42] *Tafsîr Guz' 'Ammâ*, 108. Cf. also Shihâta, o.c., 45, "'*Umûm al-Qur'ân*":
"*Fa-kull kitâb nazal 'alâ qawm bi-'aynhim . . . ammâ al-Qur'ân al-karîm
fa-huwa da'wa 'âmma li-n-nâs gamî'*".

[43] *Tafsîr al-Manâr*, iii, 160.

[44] viz. *Fu'lân*.

[45] Shihâta, o.c., p. Ṭ (preface).

monographs and learned quotations. According to Abduh too often
Moslems did not realize thet thay all were addressed by God in the
Koran, and not merely their theologians, in particular the dead
ones.[46] One can almost compare a Moslem who nowadays reads and
chants the Koran, so Abduh complains, with an ass who carries
books without being able to understand them, or to share in the
belief in their contents.[47]

The method so far discussed behind Abduh's Koran exegesis is
interesting. However, the contents of his Koran commentaries are
very much determined by what the Manar commentary calls the
"need of the times", *hâgat al-ʿasr*. Since the times are in the habit of
changing, the commentaries by both Abduh and Ridâ have lost
much of their original importance. However, in some respects they
have not lost their actuality.

At the time Abduh lived and worked, Egypt was a part of the
Ottoman Empire that enjoyed almost complete self-government.
It had been occupied by the British Army in 1882, after the ʿUrâbî
revolt. As a result of this occupation the impact of the West and of
Western ideas—but especially of Western technological and military
power—was felt more strongly than ever before. Abduh reads into
the Koran a command to the Moslems to resist this Western domination, for instance in Sura 2:(27)29 "He is it who created for you
what is in the earth."[48]

In his long commentary on this passage, Abduh writes: "Yes
indeed, the Moslems have become backward compared with the
other peoples of this world. They have fallen back into a state
inferior to what they were in before the advent of Islam liberated
them from their paganism. They have no knowledge of the world
they live in and they are unable to profit from the resources of
their surroundings. Now foreigners have come, who snatch these
riches away from under their noses. However, their Book inter-
poses itself and exclaims: "He has subjected to you what is in the
heavens." "[49]

At the time Abduh lived and worked, Egypt was a poor country.
It had been impoverished by centuries of misgovernment and

---

[46] *Tafsîr al-Manâr*, i, 448: "*wa-lâ siyyamâ idhâ kânû mayyitîn*".
[47] ib.: "*mithl al-himâr yahmil asfâr fa-lâ hazz lahû min al-îmân bi-l-
kitâb . . .*"
[48] Bell's translation.
[49] *Tafsîr al-Manâr*, i, 250.

exploitation by the so-called Mamluks, a military caste maintaining itself by purchase of new members from outside Egypt,
mainly from the Caucasus and Central Asia. Poverty and the
consequent lack of education had favoured superstition, according
to the modern apologists of Islam. Abduh vehemently turned
against the popular forms of magic, witchcraft and sorcery practised
and believed in in Egypt.[50] Sometimes his tirades against magic
(*sihr*) are more or less forced upon the text of the Koran; for instance while explaining Sura 2:(96)102, "the satans disbelieved,
teaching the people magic", Abduh seizes the opportunity to write
several pages against magic and sorcery. He concludes: "Magic is
either swindle or the result of the application of techniques unknown to the spectators."

Abduh absolutely denies the reality of magic,[51] even where the
Koran seems to recognize it, for instance in Sura 114:

> I take refuge with the Lord of the Daybreak
> from the evil of the darkening when it comes on
> from the evil of the blowers among knots
> from the evil of an envious one when he envies.[52]

Sura 114 is, in the traditional interpretation, a charm against
magic, and the "blowers among knots" are traditionally supposed
to be a certain kind of witches. Yet Abduh refuses to connect
these verses with magic, and interpretes them as a warning against
slander and gossip that undo the ties, or the "knots", of friend-
ship.[53]

No new Koran commentaries had appeared in nineteenth century
Egypt. Abduh and Ridâ, however, paved the way for the huge
quantities of twentieth century commentaries that have appeared
since and that still are appearing. In re-awakening the interest in

---

[50] Ad-Dhahabî, o.c., iii, 238: "*Mawqifuh min as-sihr*"; Shihâta, o.c., 109;
Tafsîr al-Manâr e.g. i, 399-405; vii, 311; vii, 247; ix, 45-59, where the di-
gression is terminated by the formula "'*awd ilâ tafsîr al-âyât*".

[51] *Tafsîr Guz' 'Ammâ*, 181-3.

[52] Bell's translation.

[53] In his detailed analysis of the contents of the Manar commentary,
Dr. J. Jomier touches upon the subject of magic and sorcery, but exclaims
that Egyptians might see in the Western attention to this aspect of Abduh's
reform proposals a *désir de dénigrement*. Yet two Arab scholars, Dr. Shihâta
and Dr. Ad-Dhahabî, in their respective books on Abduh's Koran commentaries, do not hesitate to repeat and analyse Abduh's arguments against the
popular forms of magic as practised in Egypt at the turn of the century. Cf.
Ad-Dhahabî, o.c., iii, 238; Shihâta, o.c., 109; J. Jomier, *Le Commentaire
Coranique du Manâr*, 260.

Koran interpretation they also established a link between the
Koran and the affairs of man's life in this world. This Abduh did
by getting rid of the weight of erudition of the classical commentaries that were too heavy a ballast even for many theologians. He
filled the space thus created with sensible, judicious, enlightened
and practical short sermons on the problems of Egyptian society
in his time.[54] In particular, he emphasizes the need for education,
the implication being that only by education could the Egyptians
put themselves in a position to oust the foreign occupiers.[55]

Ridâ went further in this respect, and enlarged the Manar commentary with purely theological technical essays that were sometimes longer than sixty pages.[56] In his introduction to its first
volume, written in 1927, Ridâ blamed Fakhr ad-Dîn ar-Râzî (d.
1209) for having done the very thing he appears to be doing himself.[57] However, Ridâ's attack on Fakhr ad-Dîn ar-Râzî is generally
understood [58] to be an attack on Tantawî Gawharî,[59] who in 1923
had started a commentary of the kind called ʿilmî, "scientific", in
which he endeavoured to prove that the twentieth century scientific
findings were already contained in the Koran. Tantawî Gawharî's
scientific commentary reads like an old-fashioned outmoded book
on natural history, which is every now and then interrupted by
verses from the Koran that are somehow associated by the writer
of the book with the particular subject from natural history he
happens to write about.[60] However, the theologian Rashîd Ridâ
must have thought it necessary to reformulate and modify some of
the ever-recurring themes of Islamic theology,[61] and though denying
the right to Tantawî Gawharî to fill up a Koran commentary with
what the latter regarded as science, he himself felt entitled to treat
of dogmatical questions in his Koran commentary, even where the

---

[54] Cf. *Tafsîr Guzʾ ʿAmmâ*, 144.

[55] Cf. Shihâta, o.c., 71-76.

[56] A list of such digressions by Rashîd Ridâ in the Manar commentary
is found in Shihâta, o.c., 238.

[57] *Tafsîr al-Manâr*, i, 7: "*Fa-huwa yadhkur fî-mâ yusammîh tafsîr al-âya
fusûl tawîla bi-munâsabat kalima mufrada ka-s-samâʾ wa-l-ard min ʿulûm
al-falak wa-n-nabât wa-l-hayawân, tasudd qâriʾhâ ʿammâ anzal Allah li-aglih
al-Qurʾân*".

[58] J. Jomier, *Le Commentaire Coranique du Manâr*, 48.

[59] 1862-1940; *GAL* S III 326.

[60] Cf. J. M. S. Baljon, *Modern Muslim Koran Interpretation*, 5:" a manual
... on biology ... ornamented with Koranic sayings."

[61] E.g. "*Usûl as-Sharîʿa*", *Tafsîr al-Manâr*, v, 168-222; "*Manzilat as-
Sunna min al-Kitâb*", o.c., vi, 154-168; "*al-Iʿgâz*", o.c., 198-229; etc.

link between the Koranic passage and the dogmatical topic treated
of was not obvious.

Abduh, with Ridâ's help, not only managed to connect the interpretation of the Koran with the daily life of the Moslems, he also
held views that were not unfavourable to the philological study of
the Koran. The philologist Amîn al-Khûlî blames Abduh for not
having realized that one cannot profit from the *hidâya*, "spiritual
guidance", of the Koran before one knows the exact "literal"
meaning of it as it was understood in the days of its revelation.[62]
But Abduh's exegetical views, especially his scepticism towards
Traditions and other extra-Koranic material from later centuries,
did not interfere with philological work on the Koran. The principle
repeated throughout the Manar commentary that the Koran
should be explained by the Koran (*tafsîr al-Qur'ân bi-l-Qur'ân*) [63]
also stimulated philological work on the Koran.

Abduh emphasizes that God in the Koran addresses the people
who lived in the time of its revelation in their own terms and their
own language.[64] Though intended to clear the Koran commentaries
from the legal and Traditional material which had crept into the
commentaries in later centuries, this maxim can also be understood
as the nearest possible Moslem equivalent of the Western *e mente
auctoris* principle.[65] Ridâ, too, subscribes to this argument: in the
last volume of the Manar commentary, for which he alone was
responsible, he rejects a certain traditional interpretation arguing
that it could never have occurred to anyone in the days of the
revelation of the Koran.[66]

Abduh's views on Koran interpretation and natural history are
not fully consistent with his other views. In a famous passage

---

[62] Amîn al-Khûlî, *Manâhig Tagdîd*, 303: "*Al-maqsad al-asbaq . . .*".
[63] E.g. *Tafsîr al-Manâr*, i, 22.
[64] *Tafsîr al-Fâtiha*, 8: "*Khâtab Allâh bi-l-Qur'ân man kân fî zaman at-tanzîl*" etc. (= *Tafsîr al-Manâr*, i, 20).
[65] Christian interpreters of the Bible sometimes adhere to the view that
Bible interpretation should be *e mente auctoris*, "from the mind of the author",
without reading into the text meanings that cannot have been intended by
its human author. The Koran, however, has no human author, but is, as
Moslems believe, the direct word of God himself. Consequently, it is not
very well possible to reject certain interpretations because the author in
his time could not have intended them: God is not subject to limitations, of
time, of power, or otherwise. It is, however, possible to reject a certain
interpretation because the public at the time of the revelation of the holy
text could not have understood it.
[66] *Tafsîr al-Manâr*, xii, 5.

Abduh suggests that the *Ginn*, intelligent imperceptible spirits referred to in the Koran and important in Moslem folklore, are to be understood as microbes;[67] in another passage, where the Koran mentions lightning, Abduh talks about electricity, the telegraph, telephone and tramcars.[68] In doing so, he too might be accused of bringing into a commentary on the Koran material which is inessential to the spiritual guidance the Koran supplies. He, however, does not, as do later commentators, suggest that these things are in a concealed way actually referred to by the Koran, or that the real meaning of the Koran could only be understood after microbes and electricity had been discovered. Abduh rather wants his readers to realize that Islam is tolerant of all scientific investigation,[69] and that the Koran is too elevated to be contradicted by modern science,[70] in the same way in which Christian theologians do not think it important whether the historical information contained in the Bible is accurate or not. The Koran, according to Abduh, is not a book on law, science or history, but the word of God: "Our knowledge of the Koran is our knowledge of God."[71]

---

[67] C. C. Adams, o.c., 137; *Tafsîr al-Manâr*, iii, 94-6.

[68] I. Goldziher, *Richtungen*, 356; C. C. Adams, o.c., 137; *Tafsîr al-Manâr*, i, 176; but here also we read: "*wa-lâ yagûz sarf al-alfâz ʿan maʿânîhâ al-ḥaqîqiyya*" etc.; o.c., i, 174.

[69] C. C. Adams, o. c., 142.

[70] *Tafsîr al-Manâr*, iii, 96; "*Al-Qurʾân arfaʿ min an yuʿâridah al-ʿilm*".

[71] *Tafsîr al-Manâr*, i, 26: "*Maʿrifatnâ bi-l-Qurʾân ka-Maʿrifatnâ bi-Llâh taʿâlâ*". It seems, however, that Abduh did not believe in the Uncreatedness of the Koran: Cf. E. Kedourie, *Afghani and ʿAbduh, An Essay on Religious Unbelief and Political Activism in Modern Islam*, 13-4 & references.

CHAPTER THREE

KORAN INTERPRETATION AND NATURAL HISTORY

Many Moslems nowadays believe that the Koran anticipates the modern sciences.[1] *"Sabaq al-Qur'ân al-'ilm al-hadîth"* (The Koran forestalls modern science) we read in the Koran commentary published by the semi-official Egyptian Supreme Council for Islamic Affairs.[2] This belief has caused the revival of an almost forgotten aspect of Koran interpretation, the so-called *tafsîr 'ilmî*, "scientific exegesis", which seeks to draw all possible fields of human knowledge into the interpretation of the Koran. Especially what one would like to label as "natural history" has taken the fancy of the contemporary exegetes who work on this aspect of Koran interpretation. In defence of the legitimacy of their endeavour to find back in the Koran what has been discovered by the sciences of the nineteenth and twentieth century, they often cite two verses of the Koran: "We have sent down to thee the Book as an explanation of everything", and "We have not let slip anything in the Book."[3] If the Koran contains everything, so they argue, modern science should be included.

On the other hand, the exegetes differ on the nature of the Book mentioned in the two verses quoted above. Az-Zamakhsharî and others assume that not the Koran as we humans know it is meant here, but a heavenly Book. In heaven, they argue, a perfect divine universal record is kept in which nothing is omitted. The Koran in its earthly form is merely a reflection of this heavenly "well-preserved tablet",[4] which indeed contains everything. Adherents to the legitimacy of scientific exegesis, on the contrary, assume that the Book in these two verses is identical with "what is found between the two covers of the Koran".[5] Consequently, they seek to

---

[1] Cf. Amîn al-Khûlî, *Manâhig Tagdîd*, 287-296; Muhammad Husayn ad-Dhahabî, *At-Tafsîr wa-l-Mufassirûn*, iii, 140-160; J. Jomier & P. Caspar, "L'exégèse scientifique du Coran d'après le Cheikh Amîn al-Khûlî" in *MIDEO* 4 (1957) 269-280.

[2] Al-Maglis al-A'lâ ..., *Al-Muntakhab*, 118.

[3] Koran 16:(91)89 & Koran 6:(38)38; Bell's translation. Cf., for instance, Ad-Dhahabî, o.c., iii, 143; As-Suyûtî, *Al-Itqân*, ii, 125.

[4] Ar.: *Al-lawh al-mahfûz.*

[5] Ar.: *Mâ bayna daffatay al-Mushaf.*

interpret these two verses as actually meaning that the Koran, as we know it, contains everything that can be known,[6] and that all sciences, skills and techniques have their roots in the Koran. Given sufficient insight, as many supporters of scientific exegesis maintain, one might be able to deduce from the text of the Koran the laws and techniques brought to light by man's scientific efforts.

The arguments in favour of the legitimacy of scientific exegesis are sometimes derived from Tradition literature as well. In support of their practices, scientific exegetes sometimes quote the following Tradition:

> The Prophet said: "There will be dissensions (*fitan*). Then we asked him: "What way will there be out of them?" He answered: "The Book of God. It contains the tidings on what was in the past. It announces what will be in the future".[7]

This Tradition at least unambiguously refers to the Koran as revealed through Mohammed and not to its heavenly supposedly complete *ur*-version, but its last phrase ("It announces what will be in the future") is ambiguous. By far-fetched explanation could one take it to be a reference to modern industrial and scientific developments, but it is undoubtedly an allusion to the Koranic announcements of heaven and hell and the tribulations of the Last Day.

Another argument from Tradition in favour of the legitimacy of scientific exegesis is the existence of medical Traditions like "He who has a sick camel should keep it away from the healthy ones."[8] The contents of these and similar Traditions and the ascribing of them to the Prophet, indicate that—though the Koran itself is not referred to here—the early Moslems did not rule out the possibility of the existence of divine "scientific" information. Even if the medical Traditions are partly fabrications by later generations and do not all go back to the Prophet, they can be used to defend scientific exegesis. It is almost unthinkable that such Traditions would have been fabricated at all if there had not been a number, however small, of genuine medical Traditions. It is, consequently, probable that the Prophet really made didactic statements on points that are nowadays regarded as falling within the range of science and

---

[6] As-Suyûtî, *Al-Itqân fî ʿUlûm al-Qurʾân*, ii, 125: "*Al-ʿUlûm al-mustanbata min al-Qurʾân*".
[7] Ad-Dhahabî, o.c., iii, 144 and As-Suyûtî, o.c., ii, 126.
[8] G. H. A. Juynboll, *The Authenticity of Tradition Literature*, 139.

not of religion. If the Prophet made such statements, there is no reason why the Koran could not have made them. Koranic "scientific" statements, however, would not have to be limited to sciences known to the Arabs who lived at the time the Koran was revealed.

In a Tradition ascribed to Ibn 'Abbâs we read: "If I lost the 'iqâl [9] of my camel, I would look for it in the book of God." In spite of the uncertainty of the origin and meaning [10] of such a Tradition, it is understandable that it is used to defend the legitimacy of scientific exegesis.[11]

In Al-Baydâwî's Koran commentary a remark occurs which is ascribed to the same Ibn 'Abbâs. In the text of the Koran we read: "Surely there is for you in cattle a lesson; we give you to drink from that in the belly of which is a mixture of filth and blood, pure milk, pleasant to swallow for those who drink."[12] On this verse Ibn 'Abbâs is quoted by Al-Baydâwî as having said that when cows are fed and their food is digested, the lowest part of it becomes excrement, the middle part milk and the upper part blood.[13]

This remark, which almost certainly is falsely ascribed to Ibn 'Abbâs, occurs in a thirteenth century Koran commentary and thus indicates that at that time some kind of scientific exegesis did exist. However, scientific exegesis, if not as old as Koran exegesis itself, certainly antedates the impact of the Western technology and scientific miracles on the Islamic world. The decisive proof of this is met with in the quotations from the works of a certain Ibn Abî al-Fadl al-Mursî (d. 1257) that have been preserved in As-Suyûtî's handbook of Koranic studies, the *Itqân*.

This Al-Mursî [14] not only finds back in the Koran the arts of astronomy, medicine, weaving, spinning, seafaring and agriculture as practised in his day, but even such things as pearl-diving. The latter, so Al-Mursî suggests, is to be found back in "Every builder and diver... brings forth ornaments", a crafty combination of Koran 38:(36)37 and Koran 16:(14)14. The art of the goldsmith

---

[9] 'iqâl: "cord used for hobbling the feet of a camel".

[10] Cf. J. Wellhausen, *Reste Arabischen Heidentums*, 125.

[11] As-Suyûtî, o.c., ii, 126.

[12] Koran 16:(68)66, Bell's translation.

[13] Al-Baydâwî on 16:(68)66; not quoted, however, in the collection of exegetical statements by Ibn 'Abbâs compiled by Al-Fîrûzâbâdî, entitled *Tanwîr al-Miqyâs fî Tafsîr Ibn 'Abbâs*.

[14] Sharaf ad-Dîn abû 'Abdallâh Muhammad ibn 'Abdallâh ibn Muhammad ibn abû al-Fadl al-Mursî, 1174-1257 A.D.; *GAL* G I 312 & S I 546; Haggî Khalîfa, ed. G. Flügel, ii 378 & vii 679.

seems to be mentioned in Koran 7:(146)148: "The people of Moses made out of their ornaments a calf, a bodily appearance". Bread is thought of in Koran 12:(36)36: "Carrying upon my head bread". Cooking is not forgotten: "He brought a calf half roasted", Koran 11:(72)69.[15]

According to As-Suyûtî, Al-Mursî had "an inclination towards solitude and disagreement",[16] which might explain why none of his works have survived. As-Suyûtî, however, seems to agree with his teachings. The fragments from Al-Mursî prove that scientific exegesis existed before the nineteenth century, although it cannot have been widespread. In the line of thought of medieval Arab scholars it cannot have been absurd. Arabic philology and lexicology had strong ties with the study of the Koran, the jurists put great effort into finding back in the Koran the prescripts of Islamic law (theoretically, but not in practice, Islamic law is derived primarily from the Koran). If philology and law, two sciences highly developped in the Middle Ages, did have such strong connections with the Koran, in fact owed their very existence to the study of the Koran, it was only natural to suppose that other sciences and other fields of knowledge would be equally dependent from the Koran.

In defence of the legitimacy of scientific exegesis, Al-Ghazâlî often is quoted, in particular his *Gawâhir al-Qurʾân*. In this booklet Al-Ghazâlî teaches that the Koran becomes transparent only to those who have studied the sciences which are extracted from it. One cannot understand the Koran without knowing Arabic grammar, and one cannot know what is meant by a verse like "Who, when I am sick, giveth me health"[17] when one does not know medicine.[18] Al-Ghazâlî uses the simile of a river (the Koran) from which smaller tributaries (the sciences) branch out. This simile is not easy to understand, but it may mean that according to Al-Ghazâlî the sciences elucidate the Koran in the same way as smaller tributaries contribute their waters to a big river, and not that the sciences are actually developed from the Koran.[19]

---

[15] As-Suyûtî, o.c., ii, 126-8.

[16] As-Suyûtî, *Tabaqât al-Mufassirîn*, ed. A. Meursinge, nr. 104: *"Mâl ilâ al-infirâd ʿan an-nâs wa-ʿadam al-igtimâ ʿ"*.

[17] Koran 26:(80)80; Bell's translation.

[18] Al-Ghazâlî, *Gawâhir al-Qurʾân*, 32 (ed. Cairo 1329).

[19] On Al-Ghazâlî and *tafsîr ʿilmî*: Ad-Dhahabî, o.c., iii, 141-143; Amîn al-Khûlî, *Manâhig Tagdîd*, 287 ff. Al-Ghazâlî wrote: *"Laysat awâʾil (al-ʿulûm) khâriga min al-Qurʾân, fa-inna gamîʿhâ mughtarifa min bahr wâhid. . ."*

The occurrence before the nineteenth century of scientific exegesis has not been noticed by orientalists. I. Goldziher does not mention its existence in his almost classical *Richtungen der Islamischen Koranauslegung*. The first scholar to have drawn attention to it is the Egyptian professor of Koran exegesis at the Cairo University Amîn al-Khûlî (d. 1967), and the merit to have made known Al-Khûlî's work outside the Arab world goes to Dr. J. Jomier who translated the article in which Al-Khûlî sketches the history of scientific exegesis into French and published it in his journal *Mélanges de l'Institut Dominicain d'Etudes Orientales du Caire*.[20]

When, however, Moslem Koran interpreters write that the modern occidental sciences and technical discoveries are hinted at, or even mentioned, in the Koran, they draw ample attention among orientalists. In his bibliographical *Geschichte der Arabischen Litteratur*, C. Brockelmann for instance mentions how Shakîb Arslân (1869-1946) *"die Laplacesche Theorie schon im Qorʾân nachzuweisen sucht."*[21] Yet Shakîb Arslân did not mention Laplace [22] by name, but only alluded to his "nebular hypothesis",[23] which, though now superseded, dominated speculation for a century.[24] I. Goldziher's observation[25] that Mohammed Abduh thought that the Koran may have hinted at the existence of microbes, became immensely popular in works on modern Islam. These observations are told and re-told, not always without an attempt to ridicule "scientific exegesis" in the eyes of the non-Moslem reader.

Hanafî Ahmad quotes Al-Ghazâlî in the introduction to his *At-Tafsîr al-ʿIlmî li-l-Âyât al-Kawniyya*, Cairo 1968, p. 28: "*Inna al-ʿulûm kullhâ dâkhila fî afʿâl Allâh wa-sifâtih .. wa-fî-l-Qurʾân ishârât ilâ magâmiʿhâ, wa-l-maqâmât fî-t-taʿammuq fî tafsîlih râgiʿ ilâ fahm al-Qurʾân wa-mugarrad zâhir at-tafsîr lâ yushîr ilâ dhâlika.*" This passage is taken from Al-Ghazâlî's *Ihyâ'*, Ed. Mustafâ al-Bâbî al-Halabî, Cairo 1939, p. 296, the chapter *"Al-bâb .. fî fahm al-Qurʾân wa-tafsîrih bi-r-raʾy min ghayr naql"*. Hanafî Ahmad understands Al-Ghazâlî as saying that "The sciences concern the acts and qualities of God"—a reference to Moslem occasionalism; the next sentence "In the Koran allusions to all of them may be found" is interpreted by Hanafî Ahmad as "In the Koran allusions to all sciences may be found", whereas it is also possible to understand this sentence as "In the Koran allusions to all God's acts and qualities may be found".

[20] J. Jomier & P. Caspar, "L'exégèse scientifique du Coran d'après le Cheikh Amîn al-Khûlî", *MIDEO* 4 (1957), 269-280.

[21] *GAL* S III 398; Shakîb Arslân, *Irtisâmât*, 117.

[22] Pierre-Simon Marquis de LaPlace (1749-1827).

[23] Ar.: *Ar-raʾy as-sadîmî*.

[24] B. Russell, *Religion and Science*, 57.

[25] I. Goldziher, *Richtungen*, 356.

One of the reasons for the intense Western attention to scientific exegesis may be found in the difficulties Western Christianity was having with science [26] since the days of Galilei.[27] Many Christian theologians felt that their beliefs were being attacked by modern science, which for instance was felt to be incompatible with the Biblical views on the creation. Many Christian missionaries must have been surprised by the ease with which Moslems declared that science was not contradictory to the Koran, that its most recent findings could in fact be inferred from the text of the Koran if properly understood, or that the Koran was not a textbook of natural history but the book of God which supplied guidance for the life in this world and the world to come, and thus could not concern itself with anything as trivial as man-made sciences.

The first Koran interpreter who treats of non-Arab occidental sciences in his Koran commentary seems to be a certain Muhammad ibn Ahmad al-Iskandarânî,[28] a physician. In 1880 he published a book entitled *Kashf al-Asrâr an-Nûrâniyya al-Qur'âniyya* (The unveiling of the luminous secrets of the Koran). According to its sub-title this work discusses "celestial bodies, the earth, animals, plants and minerals." The book was published in Cairo, a few years before the British occupation of Egypt. A second book by the same author was published in 1883, after the British occupation of Egypt, but this time the book appears not in Cairo but in Ottoman-ruled Damascus. It is entitled *Tibyân al-Asrâr ar-Rabbâniyya* (The demonstration of the divine secrets); the use of the word *tibyân* (demonstration, explanation) probably ought to remind the reader of Koran 16:(91)89 "We have sent down to thee the Book as an explanation (*tibyân*) of everything"—one of the verses from the Koran adduced to legitimatize scientific exegesis. In both these works questions of what in a primary or secondary school would be designated as natural history are superficially explained, always in connection with verses from the Koran that seem suitable for the purpose.

---

[26] Galileo Galilei (1564-1642). In 1632 Galilei published his "*A Dialogue on the Two Principal Systems of the World.*" He was tried by the Inquisition, and his book remained on the *Index Librorum Prohibitorum* for over 200 years. (Cp. Th. S. Szasz, *Manufacture*, 329).

[27] Cf. A. D. White, *A History of the Warfare of Science with Theology in Christendom* (1896); Abridged with a Preface and Epilogue by Bruce Mazlish, New York 1965.

[28] *GAL* S II 778.

Al-Iskandarânî's phraseology occasionally throws an interesting sidelight on scientific exegesis in its modern form and reveals its apologetical character. He writes, for instance, above the sections of his *Tibyân*: "Would God have omitted to reveal to the people of his Koran knowledge about ... ?"—a formula ended by the mention of some "European" invention or discovery.[29] Obviously there is a connection between the rise of modern scientific exegesis and the beginning of the impact of the West on the Arab and Islamic world. In the second half of the nineteenth century more and more Moslem territory came under European rule. Egypt itself was occupied by the British Army in 1882 almost simultaneously with Al-Iskandarânî's two publications. This European rule was made possible only by the superior European technology. To many devout Moslems it must have been some consolation to read in a commentary on the Koran that all those foreign weapons and techniques which enabled Europeans to rule over the Moslems were based on principles and sciences mentioned or foretold in the Koran.

Scientific exegesis in the modern sense is a part of the larger debate going on in the Moslem world since the beginnings of Western technological, scientific and political influence in the Arab world. This debate turns around the question whether the study of the non-Arab non-Islamic sciences from the West was admissible to Moslems, and whether the use of European technical devices was permitted according to Islamic law. In discussions on this subject, comparisons have often been drawn with Islamic intellectual life during the first centuries of the Abbasid Caliphate (750-1258). It is then pointed out that in ninth century Baghdad under Abbasid rule the Hellenistic cultural heritage was translated from Greek through Syriac into Arabic. A certain Ibrâhîm ar-Râwî ar-Rifâ'î [30] in a booklet published in 1923, warns against the dangers of assimilating foreign knowledge: only too easily are its pagan materialistic anti-Islamic presuppositions assimilated as well. His line of thought and his arguments are characteristic and representative of the thoughts generally expressed on this subject: "If only the Islamic governments", he writes, "would follow the example of the Abbasids when they introduce those new sciences into their offices and schools. They ordered the Moslems to study the Greek sciences, ancient philosophy and foreign wisdom, but they did not believe

---

[29] For instance *Tibyân* 5, 29, 132, etc.

[30] Ibrâhîm ar-Râwî ar-Rifâ'î, *Sûr as-Sharî'a*, Cairo 1342.

in them. They did not accept rules that were contrary to revelation. They disproved such propositions, for they knew that the ancient philosophers were pagans. The Moslems of those days only studied these subjects because of the use they could make of the logical and mathemathical principles contained in their materialistic and heretical systems." [31]

Ar-Rifâ'î represents those who fear "foreign" knowledge and its "nihilistic" influences. On the other hand, the opposite view is also met with, for instance in a book by a certain Yahyâ Ahmad ad-Dardîrî, a professional functionary of the Moslem Young Men's Association.[32] In his *Makânat al-'Ilm fî-l-Qur'ân* (The place of science in the Koran), published in 1945, Ad-Dardîrî spares no effort to prove the admissibility, or even the obligatory character, of the study of modern science, and this by arguments that might convince conservative, orthodox Moslems.

From the Koranic story of how Adam learns the names of things and animals (Koran 2:28(30)) Ad-Dardîrî concludes that man's vice-regency over this world is justified by his knowledge only. Man should constantly strive to enlarge his knowledge of nature and the way nature has been designed by God, according to the Koran in Ad-Dardîrî's interpretation. Ad-Dardîrî quotes Koran 35:(25)28 "Of His servants only those who have knowledge fear Allah"[33] in order to defend scientists against the customary accusations of unbelief, materialism and heresy. In the conclusion of his book Ad-Dardîrî writes: "There is no doubt that we are in a most urgent need of Arabic books on every possible field of knowledge... At the moment, the scientific level of Arabic books is not much above the standards required for a secondary school education... Maybe the reader remembers the huge library in the days of the Abbasid Caliph Al-Ma'mûn..." He concludes by stressing the need for the translation of scientific texts and the dissemination of scientific education in Egyptian society, and this by arguments connected with, or derived from, the Koran.[34]

Progressive Moslems have had little difficulty in absorbing Western ideas, but to conservatives even "foreign" information about the movements of the planets may cause difficulties. Scien-

---

[31] o.c., 7.
[32] Yahyâ Ahmad ad-Dardîrî, *Makânat al-'Ilm fî-l-Qur'ân*, Cairo 1945.
[33] Bell's translation.
[34] Ad-Dardîrî, o.c., 230-50.

tific exegesis has proved to be a channel through which those conservatives who were receptive to Western ideas could accept this "foreign" knowledge. A "progressive" like Mohammed Abduh had no need for such devices. He interpreted verses like Koran 86:(5)5 "Let man look, from what he was created?" and Koran 30:(49)50 "Look at the results of Allah's mercy" as direct divine commands to study nature.[35] Those passages in Abduh's writings that could be regarded as scientific exegesis are usually attempts to make the text of the Koran constant with reason. For instance, the famous effort to explain away the *Ginn*, the "invisible beings, either harmful or helpful, that interfere with the lives of mortals", by suggesting that actually microbes are meant, is a typical example of nineteenth century rationalism.[36]

It is true that the importance of scientific exegesis in Abduh's day was increasing, but Mohammed Abduh himself was not amongst its partisans. Its real representatives were scholars like Al-Iskandarânî, Ahmad Mukhtâr al-Ghâzî,[37] Abdallâh Fikrî Bâshâ [38] and a physician like Muhammad Tawfiq Sidqî (1881-1920), in whose work anti-Christian apologetics, secondary school natural history and reformist ideas like those of Abduh and Rashîd Ridâ all play their part. Sidqî [39] became famous by an essay which he published in 1905 in *al-Manâr*, the journal of the group around Abduh, of which Rashîd Ridâ was the editor in chief. It is entitled *Ad-Dîn fî Nazar al-ʿAql as-Sahih*, (Religion in the light of pure reason). After Sidqî's death it was reprinted separately, in 1927. It contains, amongst other interesting items, a list of forty "mistakes" in the text of the Bible.[40] In his other publications against Christianity he went so far that its representatives in Egypt felt themselves compelled to ask the authorities to interfere, "with the result that Dr. Sidkî was

---

[35] I. Goldziher, *Richtungen*, 351; Shihâta, *Manhag al-Imâm*, 71; Muhammad ʿAbduh, *Tafsîr al-Fâtiha*, Cairo 1382, 9-10.

[36] Cf., however, *Tafsîr al-Manâr*, ii, 59-61: "*Wa-hâtân al-âyatân tadullân ʿalâ istidârat al-ard wa-dawrânhâ hawl as-shams . .*" This passage seems to have been written by the Syrian Rashîd Ridâ, since it contains the following sentence: "*Wa-kathîr mâ shâhadnâ fî gibâl Sûriyya . . .*" (We often saw in the mountains of Syria).

[37] Ahmad Mukhtâr al-Ghâzî, *Riyâd al-Mukhtâr* (Cf. Hanafî Ahmad, o.c., 7; Y. I. Sarkîs, *Muʿgam al-Matbûʿât*, 399) and *Sarâʾir al-Qurʾân* (Cf. Shakîb Arslân, o.c., 117).

[38] ʿAbdallâh Fikrî Bâshâ: *GAL* G II 474 & S II 721.

[39] Muhammad Tawfîq Sidqî (1881-1920); *GAL* S III 323; Y. I. Sarkîs, o.c., 1644-5.

[40] M. T. Sidqî, *Ad-Dîn fî Nazar al-ʿAql as-Sahîh*, Cairo 1323, 11.

forbidden to write further articles of that nature."[41] Yet his attacks
on the New Testament and Paul were nothing but a reflected image
of certain now outdated orientalist opinions on Tradition literature
and Mohammed. According to Sidqî, not Mohammed but Paul had
been subject to epileptic fits,[42] and the text of the New Testament
was corrupted by malicious party quarrels, and therefore had no
value.

In an article published in *Al-Manâr* in 1910 Sidqî shows himself
an outright partisan of scientific exegesis. In this article he endeavours to prove, as C. Brockelmann puts it, *"die Übereinstimmung des
Qorʾâns mit der modernen Wissenschaft auf dem Gebiete der Astrono-
mie"*.[43] Sidqî wrote many articles for *Al-Manâr* on subjects from
natural history, which have been collected in two volumes under
the title *Durûs Sunan al-Kâʾinât, Muhâdarat Tibbiyya ʿIlmiyya
Islâmiyya* [44] (Lessons on the habits of things created, medical,
scientific and Islamic lectures). This collection of articles on chem-
istry, biology and similar subjects, originally published in a journal
which called itself *a scientific journal devoted to the philosophy of
religion and affairs of society and civilization*, clearly shows the
didactic aims of the group around *Al-Manâr* and of supporters of
scientific exegesis. On the title page of the third edition of this collection of articles we read that this book is a school-textbook, and
as such it is indeed classified in A. I. Nussayr's bibliography of
books printed in Egypt.

The link between modern scientific exegesis and the foreign
domination of large parts of the Moslem world becomes conspicuous
in the works of Tantawî Gawharî (1870-1940). Gawharî was a
prolific author.[45] Besides many other works, he wrote a scientific
commentary on the Koran in 26 volumes, illustrated with drawings,
photographs and tables.[46] "His treatment of the Holy text has
nothing to do with true interpretation", Dr. J. M. S. Baljon re-

---

[41] C. C. Adams, *Islam and Modernism*, 239-42.
[42] M. T. Sidqî, *Nazra fî Kutub al-ʿAhd al-Gadîd . . .*, 82-3.
[43] *GAL* S III 323.
[44] A. I. Nussayr, *Arabic Books . . .*, M/402-3.
[45] *GAL* S III 326-9.
[46] *Al-Gawâhir fî Tafsîr al-Qurʾân al-Karîm al-Mushtamil ʿalâ ʿAgâʾib
Badâʾiʿ al-Mukawwanât wa-Gharâʾib al-Âyât al-Bâhirât*, 2nd ed. Cairo 1350
(Mustafâ al-Bâbî al-Halabî), 26 vls.; Cf. J. Jomier, "Le Cheikh Tantâwî
Jawharî (1862-1940) et son commentaire du Coran", *MIDEO* 5 (1958),
115-174.

marks,[47] and the same feeling may also be observed in the Moslem world itself: in Saudi Arabia Gawharî's commentary was forbidden,[48] and the partisan of scientific exegesis Hanafî Ahmad docilely writes in his own commentary that Gawharî "went too far" in his scientific exegesis of the Koran.[49]

Gawharî realized that such objections could be raised against his work. He defended himself by pointing out that his treatment of the text of the Koran was not more far-fetched than legal exegesis.[50] In the same way in which the Moslem jurists built a system of law out of the vague moral exhortations of the Koran, the scientific exegetes may, according to him, deduce the movements of the celestial bodies out of the Koran. The Pakistani theologian Al-Mawdudi expressed a similar opinion when he wrote that the "sun, the moon and the stars are... all muslims"—meaning that the celestial bodies follow the laws given in the Koran in the same way in which a pious Moslem should follow the laws given by a correctly interpreted Koran. "All universe is following out the laws of its creation", Al-Mawdudi exclaims.[51] In this way, the method of scientific exegesis does not differ from that of legal exegesis, be it that scientific exegesis concerns the laws of nature, and legal exegesis the laws of man.

In 1925 Gawharî published a booklet, *Al-Qur'ân wa-l-'Ulûm al-'Asriyya* (The Koran and the modern sciences). Before turning to scientific exegesis of certain passages from the Koran, Gawharî offers the readers introductory chapters on the following subjects: "God's promise to the Moslems of control over the world", "The Moslems are neglectful in two things: unity and science", "The meaning of Holy War", "Ways of uniting the Moslems", "Number of Moslems in the world", "How to spread the sciences amongst the Moslems". The gist of all this is clear: If the Moslems unite politically and advance scientifically, they will enable themselves to throw off foreign rule. The anonymous author of the preface to Mustafâ al-Bâbî al-Halabî's edition of At-Tabarî's Koran commentary understands Gawharî in the same way: "In Gawharî's

---

[47] J. M. S. Baljon, o.c., 6.
[48] Ad-Dhahabî, o.c., iii, 174.
[49] Hanafî Ahmad, o.c., 7.
[50] Tantâwî Gawharî, *Al-Gawâhir* ..., iii, 19 and xv, 53.
[51] Quoted from W. C. Smith, *Modern Islam in India*, London 1946, 70-71.

Koran commentary", he writes,[52] "we hear a call to defy imperialism and to take up the instruments of civilization, culture and science, to enable the Moslems to resist their enemies with their own modern scientific weapons".

The first general Koran commentary in which modern scientific exegesis has been integrated is Farîd Wagdî's *Safwat al-ʿIrfân* (The best part of cognition), a Koran commentary with an elaborate introduction, now commonly known as *al-Mushaf al-Mufassar* (The Koran interpreted).[53] Apart from this work, Muhammad Farîd Wagdî (1875-1940) is the author of a ten-volume *Dâʾirat Maʿârif al-Qarn ar-Râbiʿ ʿAshar al-ʿIshrîn* (The encyclopaedia of the 14th/20th century). For nearly twenty years he was the editor-in-chief of the journal of the Azhar University.[54] He wrote polemics against Tâhâ Husayn because of the latter's views on the authenticity of pre-Islamic poetry [55] and against Qâsim Amîn because of the latter's views on the emancipation of women.[56]

Farîd Wagdî's commentary on the Koran contains three remarkable characteristics. The first is the fact that it is preceded by an essay on exegesis of the Koran in general. This introductory essay has been reprinted separately. The second characteristic is formal: Wagdî devides his commentary, which is printed in the margin of the text of the Koran, into two parts. The first part contains what is usually called a commentary; simple explanations of difficult or rare words, analyses of syntactically complicated phrases, elucidation of legal points, etc., all this under the heading *tafsîr al-alfâz* (explanation of the words). The second part bears the heading *tafsîr al-maʿânî* (explanation of the meanings). This part is in fact a translation of the Koran in contemporary standard Arabic, interspersed with remarks on the admirability and importance of the Koran. Wagdî's method of "translating" the Koran has been imitated by several later twentieth century Egyptian Koran interpreters. It is also met with in commentaries on Arabic

---

[52] At-Tabarî, *Gâmiʿ al-Bayân*, Cairo 1954, preface.

[53] Muhammad Farîd Wagdî, *Al-Mushaf al-Mufassar*, Cairo n.d., *Kitâb as-Shaʿb*, 828 pp. [1966-1969?]; *Muqaddimat al-Mushaf al-Mufassar*, Cairo 1930 (*Matbaʿat Dâʾirat al-Maʿârif al-Qarn al-ʿIshrîn*) 144 pp. Cf. Y. I. Sarkîs, o.c., 1451 6; *Dalîl al-Kitâb al-Misrî 1972* mentions four editions which were in print in 1972.

[54] W. C. Smith, *Islam in Modern History*, Princeton 1957, elaborately analyses Wagdî's writings.

[55] M. F. Wagdî, *Naqd Kitâb as-Shiʿr al-Gâhilî*, Cairo 1926.

[56] id., *Al-Marʾa al-Muslima*, Cairo 1319. Cf. *GAL* S III 325.

poetry, for instance in Al-ʿUqbarî's commentary on the *Dîwân* of Al-Mutanabbî,[57] and At-Tibrîzî's commentary on the *Muʿallaqât*.[58] Something similar may also occasionally be found in Az-Zamakhsharî's commentary on the Koran. At the end of his explanations of a verse, Az-Zamakhsharî sometimes writes: *"wa-l-maʿnâ..."* (and the meaning is ...), a formula which introduces a repetition of the whole verse that was under discussion, in much simpler Arabic than that of the original. One is tempted to call this repetition a translation.

The third characteristic lies in the contents of the commentary. Wagdî interrupts his translation into modern Arabic, his *tafsîr al-maʿânî*, with exclamations, that are sometimes placed in parentheses, such as "Modern science confirms this literally!"[59] and "In this verse you read an unambiguous prediction of things invented in the nineteenth and twentieth century!"[60] Wagdî's commentary is possibly one of the earliest Koran commentaries in which modern natural history is just one aspect of Koran interpretation. His commentary is not devoted exclusively to it, as are the works by Dr. ʿAbd al-ʿAzîz Ismâ ʿîl,[61] ʿAbd ar-Rahmân al-Kawâkibî,[62] Mustafâ Sâdiq ar-Râfiʿî [63] or Hanafî Ahmad.

The intellectual weakness of scientific exegesis becomes abundantly clear in the writings of a certain Hanafî Ahmad, who is, according to his own statement on the first page of one of his books, a *B.Sc.* from the University of Durham. In his lifetime he was an official of the Egyptian Ministry of Education. He first published his book on scientific exegesis of the Koran in 1954, under the title of *Muʿgizat al-Qurʾân fî Wasf al-Kâʾinât* (The miraculous character of the Koran in its description of things created), and he had it reprinted in 1960 and 1968 under the title *At-Tafsîr al-ʿIlmî li-l-Âyât al-Kawniyya* (The scientific exegesis of the Koranic verses which refer to the cosmos).

In spite of Hanafî Ahmad's considerable efforts, the Koran even

---

[57] Al-ʿUqbarî, *Sharh Dîwân al-Mutanabbî*, cf. *GAL* S I 142₈.
[58] C. J. Lyall (ed.), *A Commentary on Ten Ancient Arabic Poems ...*, Calcutta 1894.
[59] *Al-Mushaf al-Mufassar*, 423.
[60] ibidem, 346.
[61] ʿAbd al-ʿAzîz Ismâ ʿîl, *Al-Islâm wa-t-Tibb al-Hadîth*, Cairo 1938; Cf. J.M.S. Baljon, o.c., 89; Ad-Dhahabî, o.c., iii, 169-70.
[62] *GAL* S III 380; Ad-Dhahabî, o.c., iii, 164-7.
[63] *GAL* S III 71-6; Ad-Dhahabî, o.c., iii, 167-8.

in his interpretation contains no scientific information that cannot be found expressed much more clearly elsewhere.[64] Hanafî Ahmad tries, inter alia to prove that the text of the Koran implies knowledge of the cosmological views that are current in our days. It is a matter of some surprise that the authoritative Egyptian publishing house Dar al-Maaref, known for its meticulous editions by competent philologists of classical Arabic texts, should have published this book in which such strange philological inferences are made.

An ingenious construction around verses in which the word *nagm* (star) occurs, allows him, for example, to conclude that the Koran presupposes knowledge of the difference between the nature of the light of the planets and the light of the stars. The word *kawâkib*, which he rather arbitrarily translates as "planets" and not as usual as "stars", does not occur, he argues, in connection with *ihtidâ'* (guidance), whereas stars are mentioned frequently in the Koran in connection with guidance, for example in Koran 6:(97)97 "He is it who hath appointed for you the stars that ye may guide yourselves thereby in the darkness of land and sea". This compells the author to conclude: "Stars are the source of the original light in the sky, and the light of the planets is not original, but is derived from the light of the stars. That is why the Koran does not mention the planets in this connection."[65]

Another example of scientific exegesis by Hanafî Ahmad is connected with Koran 21:(34)33: "He is it who has created the night and the day, the sun and the moon, each in an orbit hastening on". This verse is often used to prove the Copernican cosmology of the Koran, and the phrase "in an orbit" looks indeed suitable for this purpose. Hanafî Ahmad argues that, since "night and day" cannot be imagined as "hastening on" (in Arabic *yasbahûna* which literally means "swimming"), these words in this verse should be understood as "earth and stars". Then the verse would read: "Earth, stars, sun and moon, each in an orbit, hastening on...", and according to Hanafî Ahmad this implies a modern cosmology.[66] One cannot but be astonished at this argument if one knows the rather convincing "classical" interpretation of these verses: Sun and moon

[64] Cf. J. Wilkinson, *Interpretation and Community*, 174.
[65] Hanafî Ahmad, 1968, p. 37-8. Cf. Az-Zamakhsharî, *Al-Kashshâf*, ii, 571: "*Al-ihtidâ' bi-l-kawâkib*"!
[66] Hanafî Ahmad, 1968, 287.

are "swimming" on the surface of the sky and "hasten on" like the swimmer on the surface of the water.[67]

In spite of its obvious defects, Hanafî Ahmad's interpretation of these two verses is a good example of modern scientific exegesis. Its two weak points are conspicuous. From a philolological point of view Hanafî Ahmad's treatment of the text is questionable, since it is doubtful whether a difference in meaning exists between the Arabic words *nagm* and *kawkab*, that are both usually translated as "star". Secondly, these two verses contain no information that could possibly be called scientific in any meaning of the word. A teleological argument in favour of God's existence, the so-called argument from design, may be read into them, but the verses give no information on the movements of celestial bodies that has ever been hidden from any observant biped.

Similar objections to Hanafî Ahmad's method of Koran interpretation have been raised by Egyptians. In explaining Koran 27:(89) 87, a passage on the Last Judgement

> On the day when the trumpet shall be blown . . . those in the heavens and those in the earth shall be terrified . . . And one sees the mountains, apparently solid, yet passing like clouds. . . [68]

Hanafî Ahmad again thinks that the last phrase "mountains... passing like clouds" alludes to the revolution of the earth. "This verse states", so he writes in 1954, "that the earth and the mountains on its surface ... wander through space".[69]

Four years later, in 1958, a certain 'Abd al-Wahhâb Hamûda, in an article on scientific exegesis in the journal of the Azhar University, reacts to "certain Koran interpreters" who infer from this verse (Koran 27:(90)88) the movement of the earth. Hamûda complains that such deductions do not take into consideration the context of the verses to which they are applied. An interpretation that uses these methods, he writes, "disregards the position and context of the verse it means to clarify. If in this case the commentator would read what precedes the verse and what follows it, he would perceive that the verse describes what will happen to the mountains *on the Last Day*." 'Abd al-Wahhâb Hamûda corroborates

---

[67] Al-Baydâwî and Az-Zamakhsharî on 21:(34) 33.
[68] Bell's translation.
[69] Hanafî Ahmad, 1954, 293.

his point by quoting other verses in which the Koran mentions the transient nature of earth and mountains on the Last Day.[70]

'Abd al-Wahhâb Hamûda does not mention Hanafî Ahmad nor any other scientific commentator by name. Yet he may have had Hanafî Ahmad in mind when he wrote his article—at any rate Hanafî Ahmad himself supposed the article to be addressed to him since in the later editions of his book he omits [71] the whole passage on 27:(90) 88. Since he decided, however, to have his book reprinted at all, he probably did not take 'Abd al-Wahhâb Hamûda's general criticism of scientific exegesis seriously. Apparently he did not see that Hamûda's criticism is applicable to all modern scientific exegesis and not only to his own treatment of one single verse.

There are many other modern exegetes who treat the Koran in a way not very different from Hanafî Ahmad's methods.[72] Among them we find writers like Dr. Salâh ad-Dîn Khattâb [73] and Muhammad al-Bannâ.[74] The latter is far more detailed in his findings than Hanafî Ahmad. He discovers, for instance, allusions in the Koran to aeroplanes (17:(1)1), artificial satellites (41:(53)53), interplanetary travel (55:(33)33), the hydrogene bomb (74:(36)33-(38) 35), and so on.

The obsession with the unfavourable political position of the Arab world still has its echoes in recent scientific exegesis, as it did in Gawharî's theories. "Nations are today judged by their advances and achievements in matters of culture. And this again is embodied in the Holy Quran", so we read in the preface of an English publication of the Egyptian Supreme Council for Islamic Affairs, entitled *On Cosmic Verses in the Quran*, written by a certain Muhammad Jamaluddin El-Fandy. The fact that this book was published in English reveals once more the apologetic character of scientific exegesis. Apart from the usual scientific exegesis, we read in this work: "While maintaining that the Holy Quran cannot be taken as a scientific textbook, [Al-Fandy] has yet emphasized its truthful-

---

[70] 'Abd al-Wahhâb Hamûda, "At-Tafsîr al-'Ilmî li-l-Qur'ân" in *Magallat al-Azhar*, xxx (1958), 278.

[71] Hanafî Ahmad, 1968, 333.

[72] E.g. Dr. Husayn al-Harâwî, *An-Nazariyyât al-'Ilmiyya fî-l-Qur'ân*, Cairo 1361; 'Abd ar-Rahmân Shâhîn, *I'gâz al-Qur'ân wa-l-Iktishâfât al-Hadîtha*, 3rd edition, Cairo 1369 A.H./1950 A.D.

[73] Salâh ad-Dîn Khattâb, *Al-Gânib al-'Ilmî fî-l-Qur'ân*, Cairo 1970.

[74] J. Jomier & P. Caspar, "L'exégèse scientifique...", *MIDEO* 4 (1957) 269.

ness... which is acceptable to layman and scientist alike".[75] The remark that the Koran contains scientific truth, but should not be taken as a textbook on modern science although its truthfulness is miraculous, is encountered more and more frequently in Egyptian contemporary writings on scientific exegesis. It seems to represent a compromise formula brought about by the polemics on the legitimacy of scientific exegesis. On the other hand, the emphasis laid on the miraculous character of the scientific truthfulness of the Koran caused, with some Koran interpreters, a change in attitude as regards the "wondrous nature" (*I'gâz*) [76] of the Koran.

Modern scientific exegetes have interesting things to say about the "wondrous nature" of the Koran. Their opinions on this subject differ considerably from the classical theories on *I'gâz* as expounded by Dr. G. von Grünebaum in the article *I'djâz* in the *Encyclopaedia of Islam*. The orthodox view recognized the "unparalleled uniqueness" of the Koran in its "wonderful composition and high degree of eloquence", the perfection of which mankind is unable to imitate. Many contemporary Koran interpreters, not only scientific exegetes, have some difficulty with this idea.[77] Non-Arabs, some writers argue, are unable to share this view of Koran, since only Arabs can appreciate the subtilities of the Koranic rhetoric.[78] The Egyptian Dr. Salâh ad-Dîn Khattâb goes further and even includes the contemporary Arabs themselves in the group of people who cannot (any longer) recognize or appreciate the divine eloquence of the Koran. "The majority of our generation", he writes, "is unable to appreciate the style of the Koran, because it has no thorough knowledge of classical Arabic. Therefore it is imperative that the theologians demonstrate the wondrous nature of the Koran in other spheres".[79]

Modern scientific exegetes recognize the wondrous nature of the Koran in the fact that it—if interpreted their way—alludes to "scientific" facts that were unknown in the days of Mohammed and

---

[75] Muhammad Gamâl ad-Dîn al-Fandî (Muhammad Jamaluddin El-Fandy), *On Cosmic Verses in the Quran*, Cairo 1967.

[76] *I'gâz* is the infinitive of the verb *a'gaza* ('gz IV) which means "to disable, to incapacitate, to be impossible" and hence "To speak in an inimitable manner". Its active participle *mu'giz* is translated by Wehr/Cowan as "miracle (esp. one performed by a prophet)".

[77] Cf. J. M. S. Baljon, o.c., 89.

[78] E.g. Hanafî Ahmad, 1968, 17.

[79] Salâh ad-Dîn Khattâb, o.c., 3.

that were discovered more than a thousand years later. An exegete like Muhammad Kâmil Daww writes in his *Al-Qur'ân al-Karîm wa-l-'Ulûm al-Hadîtha* (The holy Koran and the modern sciences) that the miracle of the "scientific" contents of the Koran is greater than the miracle of its matchless eloquence.[80] The agreement between the Koran and science constitutes to modern scientific exegetes a convincing proof of Mohammed's veracity [81] and hence of the correctness of all statements of the Koran,[82] including those concerning God, the Last Day, Ressurrection, etc. They never tire of repeating that it is a great miracle indeed that in the beginning of the seventh century a prophet brought a message that appears to contain allusions to sciences not developed until the nineteenth century. Earlier Moslem theologians taught that the greatness of the universe proves God's existence and implies his qualities.[83] This idea is generally met with in monotheistic religions, and is expressed in many verses of the Koran, for instance:

> Have not those who have disbelieved considered that the heavens and the earth were a cohering mass, and We slit them apart, and of water We made everything living? . . .
> Will they not believe?
> We made the heaven a roof well-preserved; yet from its signs they avert themselves.[84]

To modern scientific exegetes, however, it is not the impressiveness of the universe itself which is convincing, but the human discovery of some of the laws which the universe obeys, or rather, the coincidence between these laws and the artificial and far-fetched interpretations noted down in their scientific Koran commentaries.

Objections to scientific exegesis have been raised by Moslem scholars. It is surprising that As-Suyûtî in his article on "The

---

[80] "*Fîhî min i'gâz 'ilmî fawq mâ fîhî min i'gâz balâghî*", M. K. Daww, *Al-Qur'ân wa-l-'Ulûm al-Hadîtha*, 15.

[81] Ar.: *Sidq*.

[82] E.g. Ahmad Mustafâ al-Marâghî, *Tafsîr al-Marâghî*, xvii, 25: "*Akbar dalâla 'alâ sidq Muhammad . .*"; and Muhammad Mahmûd Higâzî, *At-Tafsîr al-Wâdih*, xvii, 25; Sayyid Qutb, *At-Taswîr al-Fannî fî-l-Qur'ân al-Karîm*, mentions three elements which according to him are commonly supposed to constitute the miraculous character of the Koran: "*tashrî' sâlih li-kull zaman*; *ikhbâr 'an al-ghayb*"; and "'*ulûm kawniyya fî khalq al-kawn* (p. 17).

[83] Fakhr ad-Dîn ar-Râzî, *Mafâtih*, v, 501; Ibn Kathîr, *Tafsîr*, iii, 177; As-Suyûtî, *Itqân*, ii, 127; ii, 134.

[84] Koran 21:(31)30 & (33)32; Bell's translation.

deduction of the sciences from the Koran" in his *Itqân* does not
mention any reasons why scientific exegesis may be unsound,
particularly since As-Shâtibî,[85] a Koran scholar who lived a hundred
years earlier than As-Suyûtî, does bring forward arguments against
it. The Koran, As-Shâtibî argues, was revealed to the Arabs at the
time of Mohammed, and was primarily addressed to the Arabs
contemporary with its revelation in their own language. Consequently, the Koran takes for granted the skills and proficiencies
known to the Arabs in those days—which misled the scientific
exegetes into believing that the Koran contains all sciences. "There
is nothing in the Koran of the things they assert, although the
Koran contains the sciences of the kind known to the Arabs in the
days of the Prophet", so As-Shâtibî writes.[86]

In Al-Baydâwî's Koran commentary a few casual remarks might
also, possibly, be interpreted as polemics against scientific exegesis.
Referring to Koran 21:(31)30-(34)33 he remarks that the "signs of
heaven" are a demonstration of God's greatness, and are studied by
the students of astronomy and natural history; in other words, not
by Koran exegetes. This remark by Al-Baydâwî is significant
because the commentary written by Fakhr ad-Dîn ar-Râzî, of
which together with Az-Zamakhsharî's *Kashshâf* Al-Baydâwî's
commentary is an excerpt, talks at great length about astronomy
at this passage.

Modern polemists against scientific exegesis of the Koran are
nowhere as sharp as Dr. Th. S. Szasz, who remarks concerning "so-
called liberal interpretations of religious documents (whether
Christian or Jewish)", that they "serve the aim of selling religion
to modern man. It should not surprise us if vendors wrap up their
merchandise so as to make it most attractive for the buyer—in this
case, so that it will conflict as little as possible with the scientific...
aspects of modern Western civilization".[87] Rashîd Ridâ wrote
against scientific exegesis in the introduction to the Manar commentary in 1927, but the first systematic refutation of it was written
by Amîn al-Khûlî, whose arguments and objections have found
wide acceptance and are often repeated.[88] Amîn al-Khûlî defines

---

[85] As-Shâtibî, *GAL* S II 374, *Kitâb al-Muwâfaqât*. Excerpts in *Magallat al-Manâr*, xvii, 273-5 (1333 A.H.).
[86] Quoted in Amîn al-Khûlî, *Manâhig Tagdîd*, 292; and in Ad-Dhahabî, o.c., iii, 154.
[87] Th. S. Szasz, *The Myth of Mental Illness*, 178.
[88] Amîn al-Khûlî, *Manâhig Tagdîd*, 290: *"Inkâr at-Tafsîr al-ʿIlmî"*.

scientific exegesis as "the kind of exegesis that reads scientific technical terminology into the expressions of the Koran and that strives to deduce all sciences and philosophical views from it".[89] This definition almost implies the impossibility of the theoretical soundness of scientific exegesis. It is literally repeated by 'Abd al-Wahhâb Hamûda and Ad-Dhahabî.[90]

Amîn al-Khûlî puts forward several arguments against modern scientific exegesis. Firstly, its lexicological unsoundness. The meanings of the words of the Koran do not bear a shift into the field of modern science. Secondly, scientific exegesis is philologically unsound. The Koran addressed the Arab contemporaries of the Prophet Mohammed, and consequently cannot contain anything they would be unable to understand. Thirdly, it is theologically unsound. The Koran preaches a religion. It brings a religious and ethical message. It is concerned with man's view of life, not with his cosmological views. Lastly, Amîn al-Khûlî emphasizes that it is a logical impossibility that the Koran, a static unchanging limited quantity of texts, should contain the ever-changing views of nineteenth and twentieth century scientists. It is not surprising that many Egyptians who want to attack modern scientific exegesis more or less copy Amîn al-Khûlî's arguments.

In spite of all this, one cannot help admiring the courage of certain scientific exegetes of the Koran. Whereas in Christianity it took centuries before the Churches "admitted" certain scientific truths, often after bloody struggles, many modern Moslem scientific exegetes of the Koran boldly claim that the Koran, the backbone of Islam, already contains the modern sciences and their principles, and all this with a courage and vigour that deserves a nobler aim.

---

[89] Amîn al-Khûlî, o.c., 287: "*At-tafsîr alladhî yuhkim (yahkum ?) al-istilâhât al-'ilmiyya fî 'ibârât al-Qur'ân wa-yagtahid istikhrâg mukhtalif al-'ulûm wa-l-ârâ' al-falsafiyya minhâ*".

[90] 'Abd al-Wahhâb Hamûda, *Magallat al-Azhar*, l.c.; Ad-Dhahabî, o.c., iii, 140.

CHAPTER FOUR

KORAN INTERPRETATION AND PHILOLOGY

The Koran is a difficult book. Its language has always troubled
people who attempted to understand it. Ibn Khaldûn (d. 1382) may
have written that "the Koran was revealed in the language of the
Arabs and according to the styles of their rhetoric; so all of them
understood it"[1]—yet the last part of this statement, "all of them
understood it", does not seem quite correct. Prophets always use
obscure language. They occasionally employ foreign words, to which
they sometimes attach new meanings, they create words that are
altogether new, and their syntax may often be called daring.
Usually, they are understood only with great difficulty, even by the
very people they address. Contrary to Ibn Khaldûn's much quoted
statement,[2] the interpretation of certain words, phrases and verses
of the Koran already occasioned much difficulty to contemporaries
of the Prophet—not to mention later generations. Koran interpretation, therefore, soon became a necessity.

Underlying the contemporary study of the language of the
Koran, two layers of ancient Arab philology are clearly discernible.
Vestiges of the past appear in many modern works which are in fact
adaptations of old forms, and the achievements of previous stages
of Koran interpretation are visibly incorporated in subsequent
commentaries. Little is dropped out of the ever accumulating
curriculum of philological [3] Koran studies; the methods of Ibn
ʿAbbâs (d. 687), Abû ʿUbayda (d. 825), As-Sigistânî (d. 942) and
Az-Zamakhsharî (d. 1144) are still in existence up to the present day.

The first layer is that of the study of the vocables of the Koran.
Ibn ʿAbbâs, sometimes called "the father of Koran exegesis",[4]
plays an important part in this. In several reports, which are almost
anecdotes, he is almost miraculously able to supply answers to
questions that are raised concerning the text of the Koran. A much

---

[1] Ibn Khaldûn, *Muqaddima*, 438: *"Fa-ʿlam anna al-Qurʾân nuzzil bi-
lughat al-ʿArab wa-ʿalâ asâlîb balâghathim fa-kânû kullhum yafhamûnah"*.
[2] Amîn al-Khûlî, *Manâhig Tagdîd*, 272; ʿAbd al-ʿAzîm Maʿânî & Ahmad
al-Ghandûr, *Ahkâm min al-Qurʾân wa-s-Sunna*, 5; etc.
[3] "Philology" is here to be defined as "scientific efforts at discovering
the purport of written or printed texts from the past."
[4] I. Goldziher, *Richtungen*, 69. Used not without irony.

quoted story, reported through At-Tabarî's Koran commentary,[5] may serve to demonstrate his fame.[6]

---

[5] At-Tabarî was born in Amul, a town in present-day Iran, twelve miles south of the Caspian Sea. His fame in the West is based on his Annals, first published in Leiden in 1879-1901. Julius Wellhausen exploited these Annals to draw a fascinating picture of the Ummayad epoch (660-750) in *The Arab Kingdom and its Fall*. At-Tabarî's Koran commentary was published for the first time in 1903, five years after C. Brockelmann had published the first edition of his *Geschichte der Arabischen Litteratur*. In his *GAL* Brockelmann classifies At-Tabarî as an historian, and amazingly enough Brockelmann's successor Dr. F. Sezgin in 1967 still discusses At-Tabarî (and his Koran commentary) in the chapter on historiography in his *Geschichte des Arabischen Schrifttums*. At-Tabarî, however, was not primarily an historian, but a theologian. O. Loth, the discoverer of At-Tabarî's Koran commentary, quotes Al-Mas'ûdî (d. 956) who has said that At-Tabarî was a theologian in the highest sense of the word. Both those occidental and oriental scholars who were unable to consult At-Tabarî's commentary, complain about this, as for instance Th. Nöldeke in 1860 in the preface to his *Geschichte des Qorans*. A certain Abû Hâmid al-Isfarâyînî (d. 1015) is reported to have said that a journey to China was not too much trouble if it could provide him with a copy of At-Tabarî's commentary. As-Suyûtî did actually consult At-Tabarî's Koran commentary and made some strong remarks on its great value.

All information which At-Tabarî gives is preceded by a chain of transmitters. These chains have been studied by Dr. H. Horst, who counted 13,026 different chains in the thirty volumes of At-Tabarî's commentary. Twenty-one out of these 13,026 cover 15,700 out of the 35,400 pieces of information, "Traditions", the truth of which is supposed to be guaranteed by the preceding chain. This form of presentation seems to suggest the sole existence of oral traditions, but after careful scrutiny of this material Dr. H. Horst concludes that At-Tabarî did use written sources in the compilation of his material. A decade later Dr. F. Sezgin in his *GAS* compares At-Tabarî's quotations with the original sources as far as available and concludes that in At-Tabarî's commentary much material lost elsewhere has been preserved *in extenso*.

At-Tabarî's Koran commentary is large and encyclopaedic. Its contents are varied and touch upon a multitude of subjects. Often the respective Traditions which he mentions contradict each other, often they are simply repetitious, differing only in the chain of transmitters. All possible exegetical problems are discussed, textual variants, rare words, parallel passages, background anecdotes, etc. In Egypt At-Tabarî's commentary has been printed repeatedly. It first appeared in 1903 at the Matba'at al-Maymûniyya, and a few years later at the Matba'a Amîriyya in the Bûlâq quarter of Cairo. Dâr al-Ma'ârif is publishing a new edition, the sixteenth volume of which appeared in 1969. A pleasant edition was printed in 1954 at Mustafâ al-Bâbî al-Halabî. (I. Goldziher, *Richtungen*, 85 ff.; *GAL* I 143, S I 217; *GAS* I 327; O. Loth, *ZDMG* xxxv (1881) 588; H. Horst, *ZDMG* ciii (1953) 290; S. Wild, *ZDMG* cxiii (1963) 289; Ahmad Muhammad al-Hûfî, *At-Tabarî*, Cairo 1962, 99-179.)

[6] At-Tabarî's Koran commentary on 2:(268)266; Az-Zamakhsharî's Koran commentary on this verse; As-Suyûtî, *Itqân*, ii, 187; Ad-Dhahabî, o.c., i, 69-70; other references: Goldziher, o.c., 73-4.

Once Caliph 'Umar (d. 644) became angry with people who answered him "God knows" (i.e. we do not know) when questioned on the meaning of Koran 2:(268)266:

> Would any one of you like to have a garden of palm trees and vines with rivers running through it and containing all kinds of fruits . . . then a whirlwind with fire strikes it, and it is burnt up? [7]

Then Ibn 'Abbâs turned to him and explained this passage as a parable on the uncertainty of man's good works. "God sometimes sends man a *Shaytân*, with the result that men commits sins in which all his good works will drown." This explanation is not philological but dogmatical. It seems to have been rather widespread: although it goes against the tenets of the Mutazilites on the necessary justice of God, it is found back even in the Koran commentary of Az-Zamakhsharî, who was a Mutazilite scholar.

Moslem tradition may have a high regard for Ibn 'Abbâs,[8] Western critics have often expressed doubts as to his reliability.[9] The main argument against him is his youthful age at the time of the death of the Prophet in 632. At that time Ibn 'Abbâs, who had been brought up in the Prophet's family, was only thirteen years old, an age considered not to guarantee intellectual maturity.[10] However, the interpretations ascribed to Ibn 'Abbâs, like the one mentioned above, often do not derive their value from the fact that they were transmitted directly by the Prophet himself to the child Ibn 'Abbâs (who, like many children, might have possessed considerable mnemonic powers) but from the threefold system he seems to have used.[11] Ibn 'Abbâs explained the Koran with the help of what he knew of the Prophet's life; with the help of Jewish-educated recent converts to Islam, who could be supposed to have a better theological training and a wider scriptural knowledge than Ibn 'Abbâs' previously pagan contemporaries, and who could often

---

[7] Bell's translation.

[8] Traditional opinions on Ibn 'Abbâs' reliability are collected in As-Suyûtî's *Itqân*, ii, 186-189. Ibn 'Abbâs is designated as *targumân al-Qurʾân*, *hibr hâdhihi al-umma*, and *al-bahr* (*li-kathrat ʿilmih*). The expression *silsilat al-kidhb* is not depreciative of Ibn 'Abbâs himself, but of some of his transmitters.

[9] I. Goldziher, o.c., 69; with references to L. Caetani and F. Buhl.

[10] Cf. Luke 2:40-52 (Jesus as a twelve year old child amazing the scholars in the temple in Jerusalem.)

[11] Ad-Dhahabî, o.c., i, 65-82; I. Goldziher, o.c., 65-81. Cp. Muhammad Husayn ad-Dhahabî, in *Magallat al-Azhar*, xxxiii, 804 (December 1961): *"Ibn ʿAbbâs, Imâm al-Mufassirîn"*.

supply the missing details in the Biblical narratives contained in the Koran; and with the help of pre-Islamic Arabic poetry.

The first of these two methods of interpretation have lost much of their original significance. The biography of the Prophet became embellished by all kinds of legendary material which was often derived from far-fetched interpretations of the Koran. Circular arguments sprang up everywhere: from a verse certain events were inferred, which in their turn served to explain the Koran. After a few generations Moslem theologians felt no need to consult non-Moslem sources on the meaning of their own scripture. They came to find the study of other religions and their scriptures to be super-fluous once Islam had found its own "identity". Only the third method, the exploitation of pre-Islamic poetry for the study of the Koran, retained its scientific value after Ibn ʿAbbâs.

The account of a meeting between Ibn ʿAbbâs and a certain Nâfiʿ ibn al-Azraq has definitely connected [12] the name of Ibn ʿAbbâs with the custom, still existing today, to attest the meaning of Koranic words by verses that were composed by, or ascribed to, pre-Islamic Arab poets. This Nâfiʿ ibn al-Azraq, a leader of the dissentient group of the Kharidjites (*Khawârig*), once came to Ibn ʿAbbâs while the latter was teaching Koran interpretation sitting in the courtyard of the Kaaba, and said: "Let us see whether that man who ventures to explain the Koran by things he does not know about, will be able to explain the Koran by means of his knowledge of the poetry said by the Arabs, because the Koran was revealed in clear Arabic speech." Ibn ʿAbbâs accepted the challenge and was asked to cite verses establishing the occurence in pre-Islamic poetry of nearly two hundred rare Koranic words.[13]

Thereupon Ibn ʿAbbâs quoted poets like ʿAntara, Labîd and Zuhayr, known for their *Muʿallaqa*, as well as Hassân ibn at-Thâbit, the "court poet" of Mohammed, and Abû Sufyân, a well-known enemy of the Prophet in the period before the conquest of Mecca in 630. An achievement of this kind presupposes a solid knowledge of

---

[12] I. Goldziher, o.c., 70: *"Eine Huldigung der philologischen Nachwelt an den eine philologische Methode der Koranerklärung fördernden Vater des Tafsîr."* And, ib., 74: *"Für Leute, die mit dieser Litteratur Umgang pflegen, steht es längst ausser Zweifel, dass kaum etwas, oder im besserem Fall sehr weniges, wirklich von Ibn ʿAbbâs stammt, was die späteren Gelehrten mit dem Nimbus seines Namens umgeben haben.'*

[13] ʿÂʾisha ʿAbd ar-Rahmân Bint as-Shâtiʾ, *Al-Iʿgâz al-Bayânî li-l-Qurʾân wa-Masâʾil Ibn al-Azraq*, Cairo 1971; As-Suyûtî, *Al-Itqân*, i, 120.

classical literature, which, needless to say, Ibn ʿAbbâs is recorded to have possessed: the historian Mûsâ ibn ʿUqba (d. 758) tells about a camel load of written notes on poetry, proverbs and genealogy in the possession of Ibn ʿAbbâs and subsequently used by his pupils.[14]

Ibn ʿAbbâs did not live in "the full light of history". We do not possess books written by him that can give a historically reliable picture of his teachings. What is known about him has come down through his pupils and through the pupils of his pupils. Apart from the clearly anecdotical report quoted above, there is no evidence that the historical Ibn ʿAbbâs did introduce the use of pre-Islamic poetry into the philological interpretation of the Koran. But even if this would not be his particular achievement, this practice must have begun very early. Few Western scholars will deny, moreover, that it was a sensible thing to do, since in several passages the Koran states about itself that it is "in clear Arabic speech".[15] Since there can be no doubt that the pre-Islamic poetry is also "pure Arabic"[16] it can indeed clarify difficulties in the vocabulary of the Koran, in the same way in which knowledge of the Prophet's life could—with the reserve formulated above—explain historical points, and knowledge of other religions, possibly, general religious phenomena.

Pre-Islamic poetry has never lost its importance for the interpretation of the Koran. To-day the custom of using classical Arabic poetry in support of interpretations of the Koran is still alive, and it may be found in a commentary like that of Bint as-Shâtiʾ. There exist separate commentaries on the verses used by Az-Zamakhsharî in his Koran commentary;[17] and the case of a certain Ad-Dimashqî (d. 993), who is said to have known by heart 50,000 verses which he employed to attest the meaning of Koranic words, certainly is remarkable.[18]

One may justifiably doubt whether it is correct or not to regard the historical Ibn ʿAbbâs as a philologist. However, there is no disagreement possible as to whether Abû ʿUbayda[19] (d. 825) deserves to be designated as such. Unlike Ibn ʿAbbâs he remained known through his own writings, not merely through those of

---

[14] *GAS* i 22.

[15] Koran 16:(105)103 *"lisân ʿarabî mubîn"*; and elsewhere.

[16] I. Goldziher, o.c., 70, f.n. 3.

[17] Cp. *GAL* S I 509; E.g. Muhibb ad-Dîn (al-Hamawî) (d. 1608), *Tanzîl al-Âyât ʿalâ as-Shawâhid ʿan al-Abyât*, Cairo 1968.

[18] As-Suyûtî, *Tabaqât al-Mufassirîn*, nr. 43; *GAS* i 45.

(pupils of) his pupils. His most impressive feat is the compilation
of the *Naqâ'id*, the polemic poetry exchange between the Omayyad
poets Garîr (d. 733) and Farazdaq (d. 733).[20] He also wrote on
pre-Islamic society.[21]

Abû 'Ubayda's Koran commentary, which was edited by Dr.
Fuat Sezgin,[22] begins with an explanation of the words *Qur'ân*,
sûra and *âya*,[23] followed by an enumeration of the stylistic peculiarities of the Koran (ellipsis, prolepsis etc.).[24] Abû 'Ubayda
contends that the Koran employs these stylistic devices in the same
way as pre-Islamic poetry.[25] After these two introductory chapters
a complete word-for-word commentary follows, beginning with
Koran 1:1. The meanings of the words are often attested by lines
from classical Arabic poetry. No chains of transmitters are given,
and no pretence is made that the information contained in this
commentary in any way goes back to the Prophet or his Companions. Abû 'Ubayda clearly offers us the fruits of his own erudition
and thinking. It is, then, remarkable that his explanations are found
back in the chapter on Koran commentary (*Bâb at-Tafsîr*) of al-
Bukhârî's (d. 870) canonical collection of Traditions *As-Sahîh*, since
this collection is commonly supposed to contain only Traditions
from the Prophet and his Companions.[26]

---

[19] Ma'mar ibn al-Muthannâ Abû 'Ubayda, *GAL* I 103, S I 162. C. Brockelmann's judgment of Abû 'Ubayda may not be uninfluenced by the former's
anti-semitism. (The *GAL* in its present form dates from the Second World
War.)

[20] Ed. A. A. Bevan, Leiden 1905-12.

[21] Cf. H. A. R. Gibb, "Abû 'Ubayda", *EI*²: "The accuracy of his scholarship was warmly defended in learned circles . . . and even his critics were
compelled to recognize the depth and many-sidedness of his learning and to
utilize his works." He wrote among other works *Kitâb Ayyâm al-'Arab*,
Kitâb al-Khayl and *Kitâb al-Mathâlib*.

[22] Abû 'Ubayda, *Magâz al-Qur'ân*, ed. Muhammad Fu'âd Sezgîn, pref.
Amîn al-Khûlî, Cairo 1954, 1962, 2 vols. According to H. A. R. Gibb, l.c.,
magâz here means "interpretation" or "paraphrase". Cf. on the meaning
of *magâz* also p. 19 of Sezgin's preface to the book.

[23] Abû 'Ubayda, o.c., 1-8.

[24] Abû 'Ubayda, o.c., 8-16.

[25] ib., Sezgin's introduction, 16: "*Wa-mâ dâm (al-Qur'ân) yahmil kull
khasâ'is al-kalâm al-'arabî min ziyâda wa-hidhf wa-idmâr wa-khtisâr wa-
taqdîm wa-ta'khîr*".

[26] Cf. on these complicated questions: F. Sezgin, *Geschichte des Arabischen
Schrifttums*, i, 83: "*Bei Al-Buhârî ergibt sich . . . dass seine Quellen zu 90 Pro-
zent auf seine Lehrer zurückgehen und dass er selten Bücher von zwei oder drei
Generationen älteren Verfassern benutzte . . .*", and ib., 116: "*Etwa einem
Viertel der Materialen fehlen die Isnade . . .*" (Cf. *GAS* i 53-84, 115-6.)

The form in which Abû 'Ubayda chose to present his commentary is still used in Egypt. In 1956 Sheikh Hasanayn Muhammad Makhlûf published a little book called *Kalimât al-Qur'ân* (The words of the Koran), which contains a list of the words in the Koran that are difficult to understand, together with a simple explanation or synonym. This book has been a great success: its sixth edition came out as early as in 1965. Like Abû 'Ubayda's work it follows the arrangement of the Koran and is not a dictionary in the modern sense of the word. It starts with Koran 1:1 and goes on until the last verse.[27]

Few manuscript copies of Abû 'Ubayda's remarkable work have been preserved.[28] This may seem surprising, but it can be explained by the rise of Koran dictionaries which, owing to their alphabetical arrangement, were easier to consult than Abû 'Ubayda's word-for-word commentary. The first of these dictionaries is the one by a certain As-Sigistânî, about whom virtually nothing is known except that he died in 942. His Koran dictionary has frequently been printed and has been preserved in dozens of manuscripts all over the world. Yet this work is, as Dr. Fuat Sezgin puts it, not more than a *ziemlich willkürlicher Auszug* from Abû 'Ubayda's commentary.[29] It owes its fame exclusively to the fact that it facilitates the access to the material collected by Abû 'Ubayda.[30]

Koran dictionaries too are still being compiled in modern times. Between 1940 and 1970 a committee of the Academy of the Arab Language prepared a *Mu'gam Alfâz al-Qur'ân al-Karîm* (Dictionary of the words of the Koran), which was published in six volumes. Among the members of the supervising committee were H. A. R. Gibb, Mahmûd Shaltût and Muhammad al-Khidr Husayn. The actual work was carried out by Amîn al-Khûlî, Hâmid 'Abd al-Qâdir and others. On its completion in 1970 the whole work was reprinted in two volumes, together containing more than 1,500 pages. In 1968 a scholar by the name of Muhammad Ismâ'îl Ibrâhîm

---

[27] A similar work: An., *Tafsîr Gharîb al-Qur'ân*, Tanta 1952.

[28] Abû 'Ubayda, o.c., Sezgin's introduction, 19-26.

[29] *GAS* i 43.

[30] As-Sigistânî's dictionary is sometimes rearranged, put back in the order first used by Abû 'Ubayda and printed in the margin of the text of the Koran, e.g. *Al-Qur'ân al-Karîm wa-bi-Hâmishih Kitâb Nuzhat al-Qulûb fî Tafsîr Gharîb al-Qur'ân li-l-Imâm Abî Bakr as-Sigistânî*, ed. 'Abd al-Halîm Basyûnî, Cairo n.d.—Cf., however, the edition Cairo 1936, 232 pp., ed. Mustafâ 'Inânî.

published a smaller, two volume, dictionary of proper names and words of the Koran, *Mu'gam al-Alfâz wa-l-A'lâm al-Qur'âniyya*. In this work the proper names in particular are treated of extensively. The interest of the Egyptian public in these and similar works may be demonstrated by the fact that the second edition of M. I. Ibrâhîm's work appeared within a year from the publication of the first edition.

These modern dictionaries are only partially the result of independent scholarship. Much of them was compiled with the help of the classical dictionaries of Arabic, such as Ibn Manzûr's *Lisân al-'Arab*, which in its turn was made with "glue and scissors", as Amîn al-Khûlî [31] puts it, out of the earlier works of Ibn Durayd, Ibn al-Athîr etc. These in their turn go back to As-Sigistânî and Abû 'Ubayda.

The central figure in the second layer underlying modern philological Koran interpretation is Az-Zamakhsharî (d. 1144), who perfected the syntactical analysis of the Koran.[32] "It is related (*yurwâ*) that Az-Zamakhsharî repented (*tâb*) at the end of his life and returned to orthodox Islam. This is indeed what is hoped for in the case of such an *Imâm*"—an unknown hand wrote in a sixteenth century Leiden manuscript of As-Suyûtî's biographical dictionary of Koran exegetes, in the margin of the entry on Az-Zamakhsharî.[33] There is, however, little possibility that what this undoubtedly orthodox and pious student hoped for actually happened. Az-Zamakhsharî was not orthodox, but a Mutazilite, which means that his theological opinions differed in several respects from what the orthodox majority of the Islamic community holds to be true. The dogma of the Uncreatedness of the Koran is the most outstanding point of difference between the Mutazilites and the Orthodox. Orthodox Moslems believe the Koran to be uncreated, i.e. they regard it as an eternal part of God's eternal and unchanging Being, a belief closely resembling the Christian tenets on the Trinity, the unity of the Father, the Son and the Holy Ghost.

"Glory to God who created the Koran" are the opening words of Az-Zamakhsharî's Koran commentary, thus antagonizing all

---

[31] Amîn al-Khûlî, *Manâhig Tagdîd*, 313.

[32] On the sources of Az-Zamakhsharî's Koran commentary: Dr. Mustafâ as-Sâwî al-Guwaynî, *Manhag az-Zamakhsharî fî Tafsîr al-Qur'ân wa-Bayân I'gâzih*[2], Cairo 1968, 79-93.

[33] As-Suyûtî, *Tabaqât al-Mufassirîn*, nr. 121, ed. Meursinge, n.C.

orthodox Moslems. Even in an edition of this commentary which appeared in Cairo in 1966, this offensive phrase was changed to "Glory to God who sent down the Koran". However, in spite of traces of Mutazilite dogmatical attitudes, Az-Zamakhsharî's work is not a dogmatical commentary. It is essentially philological and syntactical. Az-Zamakhsharî, whose mother tongue was Persian and who often taught in that language, wrote several important works on Arabic grammar and syntax (e.g. *Al-Mufassal*) and lexicology (e.g. *Asâs al-Balâgha*). His Koran commentary, written in Mecca between 1131 and 1133 A.D., presents the ultimate development of the syntactical analysis of the Koran, the beginnings of which have been observed in Abû 'Ubayda's introduction to his Koran dictionary. Az-Zamakhsharî analysed the stylistic peculiarities of the Koran and gave reasons for the apparent irregularities in the text; this made his commentary famous and valuable. He also included the Traditional material [34] and the pre-Islamic verses usually employed to attest the meaning of certain words. A Western reader cannot but be impressed by Az-Zamakhsharî's work once he learns how to use it.

From his readers Az-Zamakhsharî expects a certain familiarity with the classical rules of Arabic grammar, without which his remarks are sometimes difficult to follow. For example, in Koran 6:(2)2 "And a term is stated in his keeping"[35] (*Wa-'agal^{un} musamma^n 'indahû*) the word-order of this phrase goes against the rule that in a nominal phrase in which the predicate consists of a preposition (h.l. *'inda*, "with") and a noun or pronoun (h.l. *-hû*, "him"), and in which the subject (h.l. *agal^{un}*, "term") is undetermined, the predicate precedes the subject.[36] The normal order of the words would thus be *Wa-'indahû agal^{un}*. To view this as a problem and to understand the terminology of Az-Zamakhsharî's explanation, it is necessary to know the rules governing the word-order as formulated by the grammarians of Arabic. Any deviation from what is regarded as normal according to these rules is noticed and explained by Az-Zamakhsharî. His achievement is always to have noticed peculiarities like the one described above, even if his explanation

---

[34] According to Dr. M. S. al-Guwaynî, o.c., 89, Az-Zamakhsharî's commentary contains no Traditions not found in Muslim's *Sahîh*.

[35] Bell's translation.

[36] A. F. L. Beeston, *Written Arabic*, § 2:12; W. Wright, *A Grammar of the Arabic Language*, ii, 261 A.

of them is not always convincing to modern readers. Az-Zamakh-sharî's true scientific spirit may be demonstrated by the fact that he is conspicuously silent on the problems he feels unable to solve. This silence was not always appreciated by later students of the Koran, who (like many modern Christian Bible exegetes) felt unable to believe that the book of God could contain anything not understandable to a true believer. Consequently, they wrote adaptations of Az-Zamakhsharî's commentary in which gaps were filled and in which no word or phrase was left without a comment. Dozens of such adaptations have been preserved in manuscript,[37] and many have been printed. In these works, Az-Zamakhsharî's work is usually expurgated from Mutazilite heresies, and sometimes excerpts of the findings of other Koran scholars are also offered. A famous example of such a work is the commentary of Al-Baydâwî (d. 1286), in which the Koran commentaries of Ar-Râzî (d. 1209) and Az-Zamakhsharî are utilized and reproduced in a condensed form.

Az-Zamakhsharî makes ample use of the rather vague concepts of *taqdîr*, the supposed "implication" of a missing syntactical part of the phrase, and *ta'kîd* or *ta'zîm*, the "enhancement" of a part of the phrase. Especially in the excerpts of Az-Zamakhsharî's work which remained popular, arguments in which these two concepts figure do not look very convincing. In the condensed form in which commentaries like those by Al-Baydâwî and Al-Galâlayn present such grammatical and syntactical explanations, they often appear unnecessary and beside the point. In the twentieth century a certain distaste for the traditional grammatical explanation of the Koran is voiced in various ways, inter alia in Abduh's remarks that a Moslem should not permit exegesis to be a barrier between him and the Koran, and in his hesitation to embark upon a Koran commentary himself. Abduh limited himself as far as grammar was concerned to the grammatical contents of the Galâlayn commentary,[38] and he exhorted his readers to understand the Koran directly, avoiding the sterile scholarship of previous centuries. This slightly "anti-philological" attitude of Abduh was quickly felt to be unsatisfactory. Abduh's pupil Rashîd Ridâ already adds all kinds

---

[37] Cf. e.g. W. Ahlwardt, *Verzeichnis der arabischen Handschriften der königlichen Bibliothek in Berlin*, nr. 799 (1-25).

[38] *Tafsîr al-Manâr*, i, 15: "*Wa-yatawakka'* [*Muhammad 'Abduh*] *fî dhâlika 'alâ 'ibârat tafsîr al-Galâlayn alladhî huwa awgaz at-tafâsîr*".

of grammatical information regarding the text of the Koran to the explanations of his "Teacher and Leader" in the Manar Koran commentary.

Amîn al-Khûlî [39] (d. 1967), who taught Koran exegesis at the Egyptian University in Gîza, was the first Egyptian scholar to find a way out of the philology versus edification dilemma. He never published a commentary, but in his writings about Koran interpretation and its history he developed a theory on the relation between philology and Koran interpretation that has exerted some influence in Egypt.[40]

Amîn al-Khûlî holds that ideally exegetical studies of the Koran should be divided into two parts: (1) those on the background of the Koran,[41] on the history of its genesis, on the society in which it came into being, on the language of the people to which it was primarily addressed, etc., and (2) the interpretation of the verses of the Koran in the light of these preliminary studies.[42] Whereas Abduh, he says, attempted to bring to light the guidance (*hidâya*) which the Koran offers to mankind,[43] Amîn al-Khûlî considers it essential to establish first of all, as far as possible, the true literal meaning of the Koran, with the help of all historical and other material at hand, "even if [we] do not look for edification through it",[44] and "without regard for religion".[45] Reading what al-Khûlî has to say on this subject one is reminded of those Christian theologians who teach that "the search for a spiritual sense [of the Bible] is irrelevant till we have faced and understood the text in its literal sense."[46]

Amîn al-Khûlî clarifies what he intends to do by quoting an example of such a background study: Th. Nöldeke's *Geschichte des Qorans*, a well-documented nineteenth century work of scholarship and an almost classical example of what would nowadays be called the "traditional-historical approach" to a written text as opposed to the modern formalist, psychological or sociological approaches.

---

[39] A sketch of Amîn al-Khûlî's life can be found in Anwar al-Gundî, *Al-Muhâfaza wa-t-Tagdîd fî-n-Nathr al-'Arabî al-Mu'âsir*, 718-722.

[40] Amîn al-Khûlî, *Manâhig Tagdîd*, 302-318, "*At-tafsîr al-yawm*", and "*Al-manhag al-adabî fî-t-tafsîr*".

[41] ib., 308, "*Dirâsat mâ hawl at-tafsîr*".

[42] ib., 312, "*Dirâsat al-Qur'ân nafsih*".

[43] ib., 302.

[44] ib., 303: "*Wa-law lam yaqsadû al-ihtidâ' bih*".

[45] ib., 304: "*Dûn nazar ilâ ayy i'tibâr dînî*".

[46] J. Wilkinson, *Interpretation and Community*, 153.

Moslem and non-Moslem students have frequently judged this historical-critical method to be incompatible with orthodox Islam and with the special sanctity with which the Koran is endowed in the Moslem dogmatical system. Amîn al-Khûlî does not share this opinion: the *Geschichte des Qorans*, so he writes, is a necessary study (*dirâsa darúriyya*) [47] for the comprehension of the Koran. He argues that the Koran came to humanity in an Arab garb (*fî thawbih al-'arabî*) [48] and that we therefore, in order to understand the Koran as perfectly as possible, should know as much as possible of these Arabs and their time.

One of Amîn al-Khûlî's pupils translated the *Geschichte des Qorans* into Arabic.[49] This translation was never printed, but this does not necessarily mean that the Egyptian censors hold Amîn al-Khûlî's views and the *Geschichte des Qorans* to be incompatible with public order. In the last decades several introductions into the history of the Koran have appeared in Egypt,[50] and there is in fact little evidence of a general resistance on principle to a certain degree of historical criticism of the Koran.

Amîn al-Khûlî's emphasis on the importance of the historical background for the true appreciation of the literal meaning of the Koran, would lead us to expect a reference to something like the *e mente auctoris* principle. According to this exegetical rule, it is illegitimate to read into the text implications that could not have been envisaged by its author. However, Moslems believe that what the Koran says about its own nature is true, viz. that the Koran is not the inspired work of a prophet or apostle, but that God himself is directly its author. Hence, the *e mente auctoris* principle has little meaning as an instrument to purge commentaries from far-fetched interpretations, since it is not humanly possible to decide whether anything can or cannot be the hidden intention of the Almighty. A near approach, however, to the *e mente auctoris* principle is Amîn al-Khûlî's much stressed tenet that the Koran ought to be comprehended in the way its first hearers comprehended it. That Amîn al-Khûlî's view does indeed come close to the *e mente auctoris* principle stands out clearly when we realize that in the Islamic

---

[47] Amîn al-Khûlî, o.c., 309.
[48] ib., 310 n.
[49] ib., 309.
[50] E.g. ʿAbd as-Sabûr Shâhîn, *Taʾrîkh al-Qurʾân*, Cairo 1966; Ubay ʿAbdallâh az-Zangânî, *Taʾrîkh al-Qurʾân*, Cairo 1935; etc.

system the first hearer of the message of the Koran is the Prophet Mohammed, whom sceptical minds sometimes suppose to have been the author of the Koran.[51]

Amîn al-Khûlî's views on the second duty of Koran exegesis (viz. the interpretation of the text itself in the light of the preliminary studies) are equally interesting. Firstly, he urges the scholar who intends to write a Koran commentary to take notice of all verses in which the Koran talks about a subject, and not to limit himself to the interpretation of a single passage neglecting other Koranic statements on the same topic.[52] "In Koran 2:(28)30-(37)39 we read about Adam; but this story ought to be explained by what the Koran says about Adam in 7:(9)10-(31)33, 15:(28)28-(42)42, 18:(48)50, etc."[53] Secondly, Amîn al-Khûlî stresses the need for a careful study of the meaning of every word, not only with the help of the classical dictionaries but in the first place with the help of the Koranic parallel occurrences of the same word or the same root. Finally, the Koran interpreter should analyse how the Koran combines these words into sentences,[54] and attempt to explain the psychological effect the language of the Koran has on its hearers.[55]

We should not permit ourselves to be frightened by these tasks, Amîn al-Khûlî explains, because however heavy they are, the Koran being the greatest book of the Arabic language (kitâb al-ʿarabiyya al-akbar) deserves these efforts. "The Koran eternalized the Arabic language... and became its pride... this quality of the Koran is recognized by all Arabs, no matter how they differ in religious views, as long as they are conscious of their Arabdom, whether they are Christian, pagan, materialist, irreligious or Moslem."[56]

Amîn al-Khûlî himself never published a Koran commentary along these lines. It is tempting to suppose that he was prevented

---

[51] Zaki Mubârak, La prose arabe, 52-3: "Reste donc le Coran comme oeuvre authentique indiscutable ... C'est une oeuvre arabe, écrite par un auteur arabe ..."

[52] Amîn al-Khûlî, Manâhig Tagdîd, 304 ff.: "Tartîb al-Qurʾân".

[53] ib., 305-6: "Qissat Adam fî-l-Baqara, wa-innamâ tufassar maʿa mâ warad ʿanhâ fî suwar al-Aʿrâf, wa-l-Higr, wa-l-Kahf, wa-ghayrhâ."

[54] ib., 313-4.

[55] ib., 315: "At-tafsîr an-nafsî ..." Amîn al-Khûlî's ideas on this subject (and those of Khalafallâh) might, according to Dr. R. Wielandt, have been influenced by Al-Gurgânî (d. 1078). (R. Wielandt, Offenbarung und Geschichte im Denken Moderner Muslime, 139). Sayyid Qutb (At-Taswîr al-Fannî, 29) acknowledges his debt to Al-Gurgânî when expounding theories which are very similar to those of Amîn al-Khûlî and Bint as-Shâtiʾ.

[56] Amîn al-Khûlî, Manâhig Tagdîd, 303.

from doing so by the rather unpleasant atmosphere which was created around him in the late forties. When holding the chair of Koran interpretation at the Egyptian University of Gîza, Amîn al-Khûlî agreed to supervise a thesis offered by Muhammad Ahmad Khalafallâh,[57] *Al-Fann al-Qasasî fi-l-Qur'ân al-Karîm* (The art of story-telling in the Koran). The title of this book alone must have disquietened many an orthodox Moslem. Khalafallâh in his book maintains that the stories which the Koran tells about the prophets preceding Mohammed are not necessarily historically true. Their value, he argues, lies not in the information they contain about what happened in earlier times, but in the religious values (*qiyam*) these stories illustrate. This opinion created some commotion in Egypt, and Khalafallâh lost his position in the University.[58]

We may safely assume that we have a reliable picture of what a Koran commentary by Amîn al-Khûlî would have looked like in two books that are dedicated to him and published by his widow, Dr. 'Â'isha 'Abd ar-Rahmân, who is professor of Arabic at the 'Ayn Shams University in Heliopolis.[59] Dr. 'Â'isha 'Abd ar-Rahmân is better known by her pseudonym Bint as-Shâti', which she employs since her first publications in the thirties.[60] Bint as-Shâti' published the first of these two volumes in 1962, several years before the death of her husband. In this volume she offers an extensive commentary on seven short suras.[61] The second edition

---

[57] Not to be confused with Muhammad Khalafallâh Ahmad, professor of Arabic in Alexandria, who also worked on 'Abd al-Qâhir al-Gurgânî, and who published an attempt at a formalist analysis of Sura 13 (*Sûrat ar-Ra'd*) in the journal of Dâr al-'Ulûm, vi, 3 (1940). Cf. Muhammad Ragab al-Bayûmî, *"At-tafsîr al-bayânî li-l-Qur'ân al-karîm 'inda al-mu'âsirîn"*, in *Qâfilat az-Zayt*, xx, 3, 3 (1392/1972).

[58] J. Jomier, "Quelques positions actuelles de l'exégèse coranique en Egypte révélées par une polémique récente", in *MIDEO* 1 (1954) 39 ff.; A. M. Ahmad, *Die Auseinandersetzungen zwischen al-Azhar und der modernistischen Bewegung in Ägypten*, 60 ff.; R. Wielandt, *Offenbarung und Geschichte in Denken Moderner Muslime*, 134-152.

[59] *"Ustâdh kursî al-lugha al-'Arabiyya wa-âdâbhâ, gâmi'at 'Ayn Shams".*

[60] *GAL* S III 263. C. Brockelmann, writing in a jocular mood: *"eine wohl im Lehrberuf stehende Dame, die es vorzieht, ihren wahren Namen zu verschweigen . . ."* Nevertheless we find in the index of his *GAL* on p. 556: "'Â'iša 'Ar. S III, 263". A biographical sketch of Bint as-Shâti' in Anwar al-Gundî, o.c., 710-5.

[61] *At-Tafsîr al-Bayânî li-l-Qur'ân al-Karîm*, vl. 1, treats of the Suras 93, 94, 99, 79, 100, 90, 102 (in this order); vl. 2 the Suras 96, 68, 103, 92, 89, 104, 107. All of these are put in the first Meccan period by Th. Nöldeke (*Geschichte des Qorans*, I, 74-117). W. M. Watt, *Bell's Introduction to the Qur'ân*, Edinburgh 1970, p. 111: "As a first approximation to the historical

of this book appeared in 1966 and the third in 1968, which may be an indication of the interest the Egyptian reading public takes in her writings.

"My attempt", she writes in the preface to the first volume, "aims at applying the program [of Amîn al-Khûlî] to a few short suras in which the topical unity is conspicuous and which, moreover, date from [Mohammed's first] Meccan period, in which the Koran is concerned with the essentials (al-usûl al-kubrâ) of the Islamic call (ad-da'wa al-Islâmiyya); I attempt to clarify the difference between the usual method of Koran interpretation and our new way, which deals with the text of the Koran... according to the famous ancient rule that the Koran explains itself[62]... specialists in all fields of Koranic studies will see that we are in need, before anything else, of simply understanding the text of the Koran..." And: "Thus we will free our understanding of the Koran from extraneous elements and flaws which have been dragged into the nobility of its eloquence."[63] It is certainly true that Bint as-Shâti' in fact applies Amîn al-Khûlî's method, but there may be more in her choice of the seven suras which she selected for the first volume than she cares to admit in this preface. The seven suras which she writes about date from the beginning of Mohammed's prophethood, before he left Mecca for Medina in 622, and do not contain legal material as many of the later, Medinan, suras do. These Meccan suras may be said to be purely "religious" ("They are concerned with the essentials of Islam"), and in their explanation no points of Islamic law are involved. Nor do these suras treat of the prophets who preceded Mohammed or of the history of their times. Moslem law is generally identified with the command of God, and any possible innovation in this field is apt to attract the attention of heresy hunters. As Khalafallâh's fate illustrates, the same applies to any unconvential statement on the prophets before Mohammed. So it seems that Bint as-Shâti', by selecting these suras, consciously tried to avoid the discussion of points that might result in conflicts with more conservative Moslems. She wishes the reader to pay attention to her method of interpretation, and not to other views she also happens to hold or not to hold.

---

order of the Qur'ân Nöldeke's arrangement is useful. The criterion of style plays too large a part in it, however."

[62] Ar.: Qawlat as-salaf as-sâlih "al-Qur'ân yufassir ba'duh ba'd".

[63] Bint as-Shâti', At-Tafsîr al-Bayânî, i, 14.

It is not without hazards to attempt to read between the lines, but her handling of two topics in her commentary on Sura 93 also indicates a certain carefulness on her part not to focus the reader's attention on unfamiliar or unconventional ideas that are only indirectly connected with Bint as-Shâti''s ideas on the proper method of Koran interpretation. In her commentary on Sura 93 Bint as-Shâti' talks at length about the oath (*qasam*) in the Koran. Many suras, including 93, in fact begin with mysterious oaths ("By the morning brightness", or "By the fig and the olive",[64] etc.) that are difficult to interpret if it is at all possible to assign a definite meaning to them. In her long discussion of these oaths [65] Bint as-Shâti' does not mention that similar oaths were also frequently employed by the poets, sorcerers and soothsayers of Mohammed's day. She most probably knows this, if only because Th. Nöldeke mentions the pre-Islamic pagan use of oaths in his *Geschichte des Qorans*.[66] Bint as-Shâti' does not embark upon this problem, the discussion of which might easily evoke suspicions as to the orthodoxy of the researcher's beliefs in the Koran's literary and stylistic uniqueness, which is one of the most cherished dogmas of Islam.

The second topic which Bint as-Shâti' seems to handle with unusual care is that of the "occasion of the revelation" (*sabab an-nuzûl*) of this sura. All commentaries connect Sura 93 with Mohammed's despair at not having received divine messages for a long time. The third verse of this sura "Thy Lord hath not taken leave of thee, nor despised thee" is generally supposed to allude to a long period [67] in which Mohammed did not receive any revelation, which distressed him and made him look ridiculous in the eyes of his fellow-Meccans who had remained hostile to his preaching. Many commentaries suggest that this period of divine silence was caused by the presence of two puppies [68] which Mohammed's grand-children Hasan and Husayn had brought into the house of the Prophet's family. Since, as Traditional belief wants it,[69] angels do not enter houses in which dogs are kept, the presence of these two

---

[64] Bell's translation of Koran 95:1.
[65] Bint as-Shâti', o.c., 18 ff.
[66] Th. Nöldeke, *Geschichte des Qorans*, i, 75 & references.
[67] The so-called *fitra*.
[68] Ar. *garw*.
[69] A. J. Wensinck, *A Handbook of Early Muhammadan Tradition*, "Angels do not enter a house where there are dogs, images or defiled persons." (p. 22 & 60).

dogs prevented the angel Gabriel, who according to Moslem belief provided Mohammed with revelations from his Lord, from entering his house. Consequently, Mohammed remained without revelations. Bint as-Shâti' quotes many commentaries in her discussion of the "occasion of the revelation" of this sura, and explains that periods of revelation and silence necessarily alternate with each other like day and night (which are mentioned in the first two verses of this sura), but she does not mention that the commentaries which she quotes also contain the story of the puppies of Hasan and Husayn.[70] Only at the end of her own analysis of this sura she does briefly mention the "stories" about these puppies,[71] which are indeed widely known, but which do not, according to Bint as-Shâti', particularly contribute to the edification which Moslems may obtain from Sura 93. Besides, she adds, since the Koran itself does not allude to this story and the text of this sura is sufficiently clear, we have no need for such an addition. Bint as-Shâti' does not say that these (and similar stories to be found in Koran commentaries) are not "true". It is only their relevance to the explanation of the Koran which Bint as-Shâti' regards as doubtful.

The literary and not primarily religious or theological character of Bint as-Shâti''s Koran interpretation also appears from the way in which her two books were published by Dâr al-Maʿârif, one of the largest Cairo publishing houses. Both appeared in a series called *Maktabat ad-Dirâsât al-Adabiyya* (Library of literary studies), in which have appeared monographs on Arab poets, general literary studies (on the novel in Egypt; Thousand and One Nights; the Nile in Egyptian poetry; literature in Syria; etc.) and some volumes on non-Arabic literature (subjects from Greek and Persian literature).

"Every language has its masterpieces", Bint as-Shâti' begins her commentary, "that are considered to be the highest examples... of its verbal artistry (*al-fann al-qawlî*)."[72] For generations, she argues, students and teachers alike have been confronted in their studies of Arabic literature with the *Muʿallaqât*, the *Naqâ'id*, the *Mufaddaliyyât*, the most famous examples of wine poetry, elegies, love poetry [73] and so on, but "these preoccupations have made us

---

[70] Bint as-Shâti', o.c., 17-8.
[71] ib., 30.
[72] ib., 9.
[73] Ar.: *mashhûr al-khamriyyât ... wa-l-marâthî ... wa-l-ghazaliyyât.*

neglect the book that is unquestionably the greatest book of Arabic
(*kitâb al-ʿarabiyya al-akbar*): the Koran.''[74] In the universities,
according to Bint as-Shâtiʾ, the Koranic studies are still largely
traditional and do not overstep the limits of traditional exegesis.
However, after Amîn al-Khûlî pointed out the necessity of studying
the Koran as a literary text (*nass adabî*), Bint as-Shâtiʾ refuses to
be satisfied with the meagre traditional approach. ''But'', she complains, ''literary interpretation of the Koran (*at-tafsîr al-adabî
li-l-Qurʾân*) has until to-day remained confined to the domain of
the Koran exegetes, although it should be transferred to the prov-
ince of literary studies (*magâl ad-dars al-adabî*) together with the
Muʿallaqât, the *Mufaddaliyyât* and the *Naqâʾid*...''[75]

Bint as-Shâtiʾ proved her competence as a philologist by her
work on the poet Abû al-ʿAlâʾ al-Maʿarrî (d. 1058).[76] Also her work
on the Koran has great value. In her commentaries she always
first gives an elaborate discussion on the words employed in the
text of the Koran and their possible meanings. For this purpose
she adduces the relevant material from the classical Koran commentaries and the classical dictionaries of Arabic. The parallel
occurrences within the Koran itself, which she analyses with common sense, are to her the element which turns the scale in favour of
one meaning or another. The juxtaposition of sometimes even
mutually exclusive and contradictory meanings, which so frequently
occurs in older commentaries, does not satisfy Bint as-Shâtiʾ. In its
context, she teaches, any word can only have one meaning, even if
the dictionaries suggest that a given word may have a dozen
meanings or more.[77]

Lines from the repertoire of the classical Arab poets every now
and then render service to attest the meaning of a word in Bint as-

---

[74] ib., 9.   [75] ib., 9-10.

[76] *Risâlat al-Ghufrân li-Abî al-ʿAlâ al-Maʿarrî wa-maʿa-hâ nass muhaqqaq
min Risâlat ibn al-Qârih, tahqîq ʿÂʾisha ʿAbd ar-Rahmân*, Cairo 1950. (Thesis,
several times reprinted.)

[77] Bint as-Shâtiʾ, *At-Tafsîr al-Bayânî*[2], i, 24: ''*wa-lâ budd min fasl fî
hâdhâ alladhî ikhtalafû fîh, li-annahû idhâ kân al-lafz lughatan yahtamil
akthar min maʿna ʿalâ mâ dhakarû fî* ''*duhâ*'' *wa* ''*sagâ*''—*fa-inna al-balâgha
lâ tugîz illâ maʿnâ wâhid fî-l-maqâm al-wâhid.*'' However, in William Empson's
Seven Types of Ambiguity[2] (Pelican Book) many examples are cited which
demonstrate that this may not be true, for instance on p. 189: ''*The earth
doth like a snake renew / Her winter weeds outworn;*'' (Shelley). ''*Weeds*
mean both 'garments', especially those of widows, like the old and dried
snake-skin, and 'vegetation', especially such coarse and hardy plants as
would last through the *winter*'' (W. Empson).

Shâti''s commentaries. In her choice of verses, however, Bint as-Shâti' is not always very happy. For instance, the verse ascribed to Abû al-Aswad ad-Du'alî (d. 688) and used to attest the occurrence of *wada'a* "to leave" in classical Arabic, is of doubtful authenticity. It is found in Al-Gawharî's dictionary under the heading *wada'a*, and in Ibn Qutayba's chapter on Abû al-Aswad in his *Kitâb as-Shi'r wa-s-Shu'arâ'* (The book on poetry and poets), but not in the Dîwân of Abû al-Aswad.[78]

Bint as-Shâti' believes that a careful study of Koranic rhyme will show that no word in the Koran ever occurs for prosodical reasons only: it is always its meaning, and never its rhyme, which brings about the employment of a given word at the end of a phrase or verse.[79] Even if this is true, her arguments are rather weak. For instance, the three last verses of Sura 93 end with *taqhar* (you coerce); *tanhar* (you reject); and *haddith* (you must report). "If the rhetoric of the Koran", Bint as-Shâti' writes, "was subject to the exigencies of rhyme, then here also the last word would have observed the rhyme of the previous verse endings. Why could the text not have ended with *khabbir* (you must report)?"[80] Apart from the unconventional logic of her remark, the Koranic vocabulary does not contain the verb *khabbara* (to report) as a glance in a concordance of the Koran would have showed her. Secondly, *khabbir* does not rhyme very well with *taqhar* and *tanhar*, even if one disregards the penultimate vowel, which, moreover, would be contrary to the rules of Koranic assonance.

These remarks do not detract from the merits of Bint as-Shâti''s commentary, from which Western orientalists may derive considerable advantage in their attempts at understanding or translating the Koran. For instance, Régis Blachère remarks in a footnote to his translation of the first verse of Sura 93: "*Ad-duhâ "clarté diurne", s'oppose ici à "nuit" et n'a donc pas son sens habituel de "clarté matinale"*."[81] It is always risky to assume that a word is used in a sense other than the usual one. In her commentary on Sura 93 Bint as-Shâti' shows that *ad-duhâ* in this passage has its

---

[78] Abû al-Aswad ad-Du'alî, *Dîwân*, Baghdad 1954. The verse is mentioned in a footnote on p. 195 and designated as *shâdhdh*, "spurious". The verse also occurs in *Khizânat al-Adab*, ii, 350.

[79] Bint as-Shâti', *At-Tafsîr al-Bayânî*[2], 6.

[80] ib., 29.

[81] *Le Coran (al-Qur'ân) traduit de l'arabe par Régis Blachère, Professeur à la Sorbonne*, Paris 1957, p. 655.

usual meaning of morning brightness, and she shows how the mis-
understanding from which also Régis Blachère suffered arose. In
the second verse of this sura Régis Blachère again becomes the
victim of an ancient confusion in the classical Koran commentaries.
He translates the verse as *"Par la Nuit quand elle règne"*—and it is
true that "to reign" sounds a very fitting thing for a night to do.
Except for the euphony of the French language, however, there
are but few reasons to stick to this translation. Bint as-Shâti' explains in her commentary why the classical dictionaries hesitate
when rendering the meaning of *sagâ*, the word translated as *règne*
by Régis Blachère, which occurs only once in the Koran. The context compels her to conclude that the word actually means "to be
quiet". Finally, her discussion of the word *âkhira* "hereafter" or
"future" (employed in the fourth verse of Sura 93) is also illuminating. With the help of Koranic parallel occurrences and the
context of this particular passage she ascertains that this word has
not necessarily eschatological connotations and may simply mean
"the future".

The examples cited hitherto may create the impression that like
her predecessors Ibn 'Abbâs and As-Sigistânî, Bint as-Shâti' is
primarily interested in establishing the exact meaning of every
single word in the Koran. This impression, however, would not be
correct. Bint as-Shâti''s ambitions go further than the vocables of
the Koran. She has an open eye for the division into pericopes,
their internal structure and their relation to each other. That Bint
as-Shâti''s interest goes further than the vocabulary of the Koran
can be illustrated by the theory which she expounds on the oath
(*qasam*) in the Koran.

Usually these mysterious oaths, which occur at the beginning of
some suras, are understood as divine indications of the greatness
of the objects sworn by, *"li-Ta'zîm al-Makhlûqât"*, "to enhance the
grandeur of things created". This theory, accepted by such authorities as Ibn Qayyim al-Gawziyya (d. 1350) and Mohammed Abduh
(d. 1905) is not satisfactory, according to Bint as-Shâti'. When the
Koran wishes to emphasize God's greatness by pointing to the
greatness of his creation, this is done explicitly. The mere mentioning in the mysterious oaths of things created (even the creation
of the smallest thing is a great miracle) is not to be equalled to
those passages in which the magnificence of the Creator is inferred
from the magnificence of his creation.

Accordingly, Bint as-Shâti' considers the oath in the Koran to be a stylistic device to draw attention as forcefully as possible to something which is open to sensory perception [82] and has some characteristics in common with something which is spiritual [83] and which is not expressed in the oath itself. Oaths mentioning day and light point to revelation and divine guidance; oaths mentioning night and darkness are to be associated with error and paganism, according to this theory, which Bint as-Shâti' claims to be original. [84]

In the case of Sura 93, Bint as-Shâti' explains that in the first two verses the Koran mentions two alternating phenomena: "By the *morning* brightness, by the *night* when it is quiet." In the next three verses again two necessarily alternating phenomena are mentioned: periods of divine silence and periods of revelation. In the verses 6-8 of this sura, moreover, the periodic fluctuations of man's material position are emphasized. In the case of Sura 79 Bint as-Shâti''s theory offers an attractive solution to the problem of the very curious oaths at the beginning of this sura:

> Drawing full stretch
> Hustling and bustling
> Toiling and moiling
> Striving to be the foremost
> Managing affairs
> —On the Day when the quake shall come. [85]

Bint as-Shâti' takes these verses as a description of the Day of Judgment—here she agrees with all other commentators—and she wishes to understand the first five verses as a description of a concrete phenomenon, viz. the roaring of the hoofs of a herd of horses. [86] The Arabic text with its feminine plural participles admits of this explanation, and the sound of a herd of horses, though little heard in modern cities, is indeed a fitting simile for the Last Day. It may have impressed the unbelieving Meccans, to which this sura was addressed, more than the description of the angels, whom Al-Baydâwî here considers to be invoked in order to impress them.

Bint as-Shâti' does not claim to dictate the final truth about the "real" meaning of the Koran, but the benefits one may obtain from studying the works of Bint as-Shâti' and Amîn al-Khûlî will

---

[82] Ar. *hissî*.
[83] Ar. *ma'nawî*.
[84] Bint as-Shâti', *At-Tafsîr al-Bayânî* [2], i, 18-23.
[85] Bell's translation.
[86] Bint as-Shâti', *At-Tafsîr al-Bayânî* [2], i, 137 ff.

certainly equal if not surpass the benefits obtainable from the classical Koran commentaries, the importance of which would sometimes seem to have been overrated by Western scholars.

Not all modern philological commentaries are as interesting as those by Bint as-Shâti'. Many modern "philological" commentators confine themselves to copying the works of Az-Zamakhsharî (d. 1144) or, worse still, copying one of his imitators. Pure philological commentaries, moreover, are rare. Most commentaries are of a mixed nature, but all works on the Koran contain extensive philological discussions. Even a commentary devoted to the correspondences between the Koran and modern "science", like the work by Hanafî Ahmad, contains more or less "philological" sections. In school-books and popular Koran commentaries much attention is indeed paid to the philology of the Koran. The fact that the treatment of philological matters is almost entirely traditional and depends upon Az-Zamakhsharî, may perhaps account for the fact that among modern Moslem scholars little independent research on the philological problems of the Koran has been conducted as yet. Still, one should bear in mind that the average contemporary Egyptian Moslem, thanks to his primary and secondary education, is better acquainted with the philological problems raised by the Koran, than the average occidental Christian with the textual and philological problems of the Bible.

CHAPTER FIVE

PRACTICAL KORAN INTERPRETATION

Rashîd Ridâ (d. 1935), Abduh's "leading pupil",[1] is commonly regarded as the first heir [2] of Abduh in the matter of the practical exegesis of the Koran. Yet, as has been pointed out above,[3] there are differences between Abduh's and Ridâ's exegetical work. This is admitted by Rashîd Ridâ himself when he writes about his own activities: "When I had to work independently after the death of Abduh, I diverged from his method by treating of the text of the Koran in a more elaborate way [4]... I endeavoured to solve ancient controversies that have divided the *'Ulamâ'*... I devoted more attention to questions the solution of which is eagerly sought by the Moslems of to-day..."[5]

However, in reality it was Muhammad Mustafâ al-Marâghî [6] (d. 1945) on whom the largest portion of Abduh's mantle fell. Like Abduh, Al-Marâghî was a member of a committee for the reform of the Azhar University (*Lagnat Islâh al-Azhar*).[7] The work of this committee resulted in the promulgation of the law of 16th November 1930, which, inter alia, divided the Azhar into three faculties: Islamic law or *sharî'a*, theology or *usûl ad-dîn*, and the Arabic language, *al-lugha al-'arabiyya*.[8] Al-Marâghî was twice rector of the Azhar: from May 1928 to October 1929, and from April 1935 until his death on 22nd August 1945.[9] Unlike Ridâ, he considered the

---

[1] So according to C. C. Adams, *Islam and Modernism*, 177.

[2] 'Abd al-'Azîm Ahmad al-Ghubâshî, *Ta'rîkh at-Tafsîr*, 163: *al-wârith al-awwal* . . .

[3] cf. p. 32.

[4] Ar.: *lammâ istaqlaltu bi-l-'amal . . . khâlaftu manhagah . . . bi-t-tawassu'* . . .

[5] *Tafsîr al-Manâr*, i, 16 (Rashîd Ridâ's introduction).

[6] Not to be confused with Ahmad Mustafâ al-Marâghî, teacher at *Dâr al-'Ulûm*, who wrote an elaborate, complete, mainly philological Koran commentary in 1945. The third edition of this work appeared in 1962, in thirty volumes, each of about 200 pages. Its title is simply *Tafsîr al-Marâghî*. Although the preface does not say so, the commentary was probably written for the students of *Dâr al-'Ulûm*, as the style and contents indicate. It is a lucid but not original work.

[7] Cf. Anwar al-Gundî, *Tarâgim al-A'lâm al-Mu'âsirîn*, 430 ff.

[8] Cf. also *EI*[2], "Azhar", i, 818.

[9] Anwar al-Gundî, ib., 431.

translation of the Koran as permissible.[10] Like later conservative reformers, his interest in Islamic law as a legal system in the Western sense of the word was limited. For instance, he declined to be classified as a member of any one of the four orthodox schools (*madhâhib*) of Islamic law.[11]

Like Abduh, he did not embark upon a complete commentary of the Koran, but produced a small amount of exegetical lectures on a few selected verses from the Koran.[12] Some of these were not published by Al-Marâghî himself, but by younger collaborators like Farîd Wagdî and Mahmûd Shaltût. These lectures, originally delivered in mosques in Cairo during Ramadân in the years 1937-43, read more like sermons than like exegesis. They seem to have been broadcast by radio and to have been extremely popular in their time.

Al-Marâghî considered it useful to point to the greatness of creation in order to illustrate the greatness of the Creator. Also, he regarded a superficial knowledge of the "modern sciences" as a necessary prerequisite of a contemporary exegete of the Koran.[13] However, he rejects scientific exegesis: "Moslems used to debate on the creed and on Islamic law; nowadays, however, another disease (*marad âkhar*) has smitten them: they want to elucidate the Koran in accordance with scientific theories that may or may not prove to be true... this is a great danger to the Book... these theories are not fit to be drawn into the explanation of the Koran".[14]

Since Al-Marâghî's exegetical lectures were usually held during

---

[10] Cf. M. M. al-Marâghî, *Bahth fî Targamat al-Qurʾân wa-Ahkâmhâʾ* Cairo 1355/1936.

[11] Cf. e.g. Ad-Dhahabî, *At-Tafsîr wa-l-Mufassirûn*, iii, 272: *lâ yaqif ʿind madhhab makhsûs*. The statements by present-day reformers as to their unwillingness to adhere to any *madhhab* (school of Islamic law) should only be interpreted as an indication of a certain distaste for an entirely legalistic interpretation of Islam and its doctrine of duties. It does not mean that they, for instance, do not say their prayers according to Shâfiʿi or Hanafî law.

[12] A complete bibliography of these lectures, which have so far not been collected in one volume, may be found with Ad-Dhahabî, o.c., iii, 257-260. Al-Marâghî talked on Koran 42:13-4 (1356); 6:151-3 (1356); 2:183-6 (1356); 8:24-9 (1357); 49 (1358); 57 (1359); 31 (1360); 6:160-5 (1361); 7:199-206 (1361); 41:30-4 (1361); 7:1-9 (1362); 11:112-123 (1362); 4:58-9 (1363); 13:17 (1363); 28:83-8 (1363); 25:1-10 (1360); 25:63-77 (1359); 103 (1361). The last three of these lectures were held at meetings of the Moslem Young Men's Association.

[13] M. M. al-Marâghî, *Tafsîr Sûrat Luqmân*, 12. (Koran 31). (*Ad-Durûs ad-Dîniyya*).

[14] M. M. al-Marâghî, *Tafsîr Sûrat al-Hugurât*, 42. (Koran 49). (*Ad-Durûs ad-Dîniyya*).

Ramadân, the Moslem month of fasting, large parts of them are concerned with fasting and its merits. Yet their contents and style are typical of later sermon-like Koran interpretation, like the works of Sayyid Qutb [15] and Mahmûd Shaltût. For instance Al-Marâghî quickly arrives at edifying generalities when he talks about Koran 2:(179)183 "O ye who have believed, fasting is prescribed for you..."[16]

Here Al-Marâghî writes: "Fasting is one of the five pillars of Islam. It is a bodily and moral exercise and spiritual purification. To persist in physical desires... prevents the acquisition of divine inspiration and the pleasure of communion with God... In our life on this world everything is possible: poverty after wealth, sickness after health, insignificance after celebrity... when misfortune strikes, one needs to be fortified against it... so, in his wisdom God made the acts of devotion a means of strengthening body and mind...",[17] and so on. There is little in these sermons that could not just as well have been said by a Christian preacher eager to strengthen the souls of his believers.[18]

Practical edifying exegesis is produced in huge quantities, even by Amîn al-Khûlî,[19] who, in the years 1941-2, gave lectures which were broadcast on the Egyptian radio, on subjects from the Koran. He himself called these sermons "an echo of literary exegesis".[20] Al-Khûlî did not talk about single words or verses in these lectures, nor even about single suras or groups of suras, since he regarded doing so as "not fitting the importance of the Book",[21] but he applied his method to general topics ("what mission have we in this world?") which are treated throughout the Koran.[22] Sometimes

---

[15] Sayyid Qutb's Koran commentary (Fî Zilâl al-Qurʾân, In the shadows of the Koran, thirty volumes, each comprising about 200 pages) is hardly a commentary of the Koran in the strict sense of the word, but rather an enormous collection of sermons.

[16] Bell's translation.

[17] Ad-Dhahabî, o.c., 263. These quotations were taken from Al-Marâghî's exegetical lecture held in Ramadân 1357, p. 6-7.

[18] The same applies to preachers like Dr. B. Graham. Apart from a small number of proper names of Palestinians which Dr. B. Graham usually drops at the end of his speeches, most of his words are of so general a nature that they could equally be said by a preacher in the Azhar.

[19] Cf. Amîn al-Khûlî's Min Hudâ al-Qurʾân.

[20] Amîn al-Khûlî, Min Hudâ al-Qurʾân: al-Qâda ... ar-Rusul, 8: "sadâ li-t-Tafsîr al-adabî".

[21] ib., 11: "dhâlika lâ yulâʾim ahammiyat al-Kitâb ..."

[22] ib., 10.

such exegetical sermons treat in a more or less allusive manner the burning topics of the day the free discussion of which is for political reasons not permitted by the government. An example of this last category may be found in the exegetical articles published in the Cairo daily newspaper [23] *Al-Gumhûriyya* by a certain 'Abd ar-Rahmân al-Bannâ', in 1959.

In the last days of November 1959 this 'Abd ar-Rahmân al-Bannâ', a brother of the founder of the Society of the Moslem Brothers (*Gam'iyyat Al-Ikhwân al-Muslimîn*) [24] started a semi-daily column in *Al-Gumhûriyya*. In these short articles he offered an interpreta-

---

[23] Most Egyptian newspapers regularly publish articles on the Koran or Koran interpretation. For instance, in *Al-Ahrâm* it is Bint as-Shâti' who is responsible for these articles.

[24] The religious associations in Egypt are usually well-controlled by the Government. The mystical fraternities, the youth organizations and the Azhar sheikhs have practically always loyally attended to the orders of the successive Egyptian governments. The one exception to this compliance is the Society of the Moslem Brothers, about which the American historian and orientalist Dr. R. P. Mitchell published a comprehensive study in 1969.

The history of the Society is full of struggle, antagonism, assaults and executions. Its founder Hasan al-Bannâ' was killed (allegedly by a government agent) on 12th February 1949, after the murder of the then Prime Minister An-Nuqrashî Pâshâ on 12th December 1948 by a member of the Society, the 23 year old veterinary student 'Abd al-Magîd Hasan, who was executed for his deed on 25th April 1950. The Nasser Government hanged six members of the Society on 9th December 1954, after an attempt on the life of Nasser on 27th October 1954; after an alleged conspiracy against Nasser's Government in 1965 and 1966, three more members of the Society were hanged on 29th August 1966, one of whom was Sayyid Qutb.

These executions were only the peak of an iceberg: hundreds of "Brothers" have languished in labour camps and prisons. Almost since its foundation (1928) the Society of the Moslem Brothers has been involved in a tenacious struggle with the successive governments, the only exception being the "short honeymoon" immediately after the rise to power of Nasser's Free Officers. This period of good relations between the Government and the Society was due to the contacts which the Free Officers had had with the Society (as with other organizations, e.g. the Wafdists and Communists) before their *coup d'état* in July 1952. The Brothers seem more or less to have promised to support the Junta government of Neguib and Nasser.

Yet after the 1952 Revolution the relations between the Government and the Society quickly became strained again. In the summer of 1954 the tension rose high, which culminated in the attempt on Nasser's life in October. During that eventful year, one faction in the Society, led by 'Abd ar-Rahmân al-Bannâ', a brother of the founder of the Society, still "was prepared to support the junta". According to Dr. Mitchell this could be explained partly by an animosity between the then leader of the Society, the ex-judge al-Hudaybî, and 'Abd ar-Rahmân al-Bannâ', who was, in Dr. Mitchell's words, a "semi-partisan" of Nasser (Cf. Richard P. Mitchell, *The Society of the Muslim Brothers*, London 1969).

tion of Sura 49, in which the Koran talks about discord in the Moslem community. Each verse of this sura was discussed in more than one article, for instance verse 9 was treated on 26th, 27th, 29th and 30th November:

> If two parties of believers fight, set things right between them, and if one of the parties is outrageous to the other, fight the one which is outrageous until it returns to the affair of Allah;
> then if it returns, set things right between them justly, and act fairly;
> Allah loveth those who act fairly.[25]

In the first article ʿAbd ar-Rahmân al-Bannâʾ points to the blood-thirsty anarchy in the days before the advent of Islam. He praises the Prophet for establishing order in the chaotic Arabian peninsula in the seventh century A.D. The article does not differ much from the usual apologetics on this theme, but it is phrased in a way which makes it almost impossible not to be reminded of the anarchy prevailing in Egypt in the years before the Nasser-régime came to power, the internal peace the régime managed to bring about, and the trouble the Government had in suppressing the activities of the fanatics amongst the Society of the Moslem Brothers. Al-Bannâʾ writes:

> [When Islam came] order was finally established, laws were enacted, mankind came to know what life really is; . . . "If two parties of the believers fight, set things right between them", certainly! To prevent bloodshed! And to protect their rights! To defend their lives! To bring order to that corrupt and harmful anarchy! It was a duty to the believers to stop the outrageous, to restrain those who transgressed the limits set by justice, and to bring back those who strayed away from probity. Nobody and nothing could be secure until "things were set right between the people justly." That is part of what this verse means. Nothing could be more correct and nothing could give better spiritual guidance. . .

In the second article the author explains that the verse about which he writes may also apply to individuals who rebel against other believers because "a party may consist of one member only". It also applies, so he continues, to groups of which only one member commits unjust acts: "The believers are like one body, if one of its members suffers from something, this causes the other members insomnia and fever." Reading these remarks, one cannot but be

---

[25] Bell's translation (adapted).

reminded of the successive statements by Hasan al-Bannâ', the
one-time leader of the Society of the Moslem Brothers, in which the
responsibility of the Society for acts of terrorism committed by
individual members was denied. This happened, for instance after
the murder, by members of the Society, of Nuqrashî Pâshâ in 1948;
and a similar situation occurred in 1954, when the leadership of
the Society was not in touch with the activities of those Brothers
who on 27th October made an attempt on the life of Nasser.[26]
'Abd ar-Rahmân who, as a member of the Society may have suffered some insomnia in these periods, concludes his article as follows:

> When quarrels arise or fighting breaks out in the Moslem commu-
> nity . . . it is the duty of all believers to hasten to interfere and "to
> set things right" quickly. To preserve peace in the land of the faith-
> ful is a binding obligation. The land of the faithful is united by one
> creed: "This community of you is one community; I am your Lord
> so show piety towards Me."

This last quotation from the Koran is interesting. Those of Al-
Bannâ''s readers who knew the Koran by heart will no doubt have
realized that the verse cited here continues with: "But they cut
their affair to pieces amongst them . . . leave them in their confusion for a time."[27]

It is not explicit whether the government or the Society of the
Moslem Brothers should be left in confusion, "cutting its affair to
pieces", but Al-Bannâ''s readers may have had definite ideas on
this subject. In the third article Al-Bannâ' emphasizes that the
Koran applies the word "believers" to both parties that are fighting
each other: "If two parties of the *believers* fight", so the text runs.
"They are our brothers who outraged us", Al-Bannâ' writes, "but
this must not be a reason for the degeneration of our belief. . . on
the contrary, it should cause us to adhere more firmly to the Book
of God." It is difficult not to understand these phrases as an allusion
to the tribulations the members of the Society of the Moslem
Brothers were going through after the government had decided to
extirpate their organization.[28]

---

[26] Cf. R. P. Mitchell, o.c., 70 & 76.
[27] Bell's translation.
[28] Cf. R. P. Mitchell, o.c.—Al-Bannâ''s articles were collected in *Min
Ma'ânî al-Qur'ân, Tafsîr Sûrat al-Hugurât*, Cairo n.d., from which the above
quotations were drawn. Egyptian politics are complicated and not easy to
understand. The number of people outside Egypt who are able to decode

The religious organizations in Egypt are large in number. Every town or neighbourhood has its mystical fraternities or branches of the Moslem Young Men's Association. The religious organizations publish in their often stencilled periodicals exegetical lectures which are either excerpts of older commentaries or sermon-like. They are often allusive to events contemporary with their publication and hence hard to understand.[29] The leaders of these organizations, however, are not very eager, to say the least, to distribute their publications amongst non-members—let alone orientalists. One is obliged to respect this unwillingness, and can only hope that especially the sermon-like exegesis of the Koran which some of these publications contain will be used by historians and sociologists who describe the teachings and activities of these organizations.

The most important aspect of Islamic religious practice, is not the sermon, the recitation of the Koran,[30] or the activities of the

---

cryptic references in Koran commentaries to current controversial topics is not large. That it is possible to do so in the case of Al-Bannâ''s work is due exclusively to Dr. R. P. Mitchell's publication on the Society of the Moslem Brothers and the comparative simplicity of Al-Bannâ''s allusions.

[29] Based on oral information from Ahmad Yûsuf (Gîza) and the book-seller Zâki Mugâhid (Cairo), orally confirmed by Mr. F. de Jong (Leiden) who spent the years 1969-72 in Egypt studying the mystical fraternities.

[30] The efforts devoted to Koran recitation throw light on the awe in which Moslems hold the Koran, and this awe in its turn is an (often acknowledged) motive underlying the exegetical work on the Koran. (Cp. Sayyid Qutb, *At-Taswîr al-Fannî*). In their private life, Moslems recite fragments from the Koran in their daily prayers, and in the prayers said at burials, marriage ceremonies, births, etc. However, the recitation of the Koran may also, on these occasions, be performed by professionals. To become a professional reciter, two qualifications are necessary: to have a good voice and to know the Koran by heart. There exists an Azhar diploma for professional reciters. On this diploma and the examination the American orientalist Dr. M. Berger wrote a moving description in his *Islam in Egypt Today*, p. 12-3:

> With the diploma, the reciter is eligible to become a muezzin or a reciter of the Koran before the Friday prayer. Candidates who want the Al-Azhar diploma must sit for an examination by a five-man committee which, when I observed its work, was composed of three venerable Al-Azhar shaikhs, an official of the Ministry of Waqfs, and a secular musical expert who had been the president of the Institute of Arab Music (as well as a highly capable amateur player of oriental music, a judge, and a lay psychologist). The committee met regularly and frequently in the office of the Ministry official, where I observed its procedures many times. The candidates gathered in the corridor, and one was called in at a time. He would remove his shoes and sit cross-legged on a straight-backed chair. The examiners would ask him to recite various passages of the Koran for ten to twenty minutes. Meanwhile, in the oriental manner, the ordinary affairs conducted in

religious organizations. The whole of Islamic religious practice is found in the Islamic "doctrine of duties", a term which C. Snouck Hurgronje, a Dutch orientalist, introduced to render the Arabic word *fiqh*. *Fiqh* embraces all aspects of life: prayer, pilgrimage, marriage, wills, trade and even food. It is conventionally divided by Moslems into two parts: the *ʿibâdât*, laws regulating ritual and religious observances, and the *muʿâmalât*, laws for the questions that arise between people in daily life. Contrary to what is the case in Western systems of law, *fiqh* also pays elaborate attention to the moral side of an act: all acts are classified as (1) obligatory; (2) desirable; (3) indifferent; (4) reprehensible; (5) forbidden.[31]

The prescripts of Islamic law are generally identified with the command of God. Yet the role in Islamic law of God's word, the Koran, is much smaller than is usually supposed.[32] In a common handbook on the "roots" of the law, the space devoted to the discussion of the Koran as a source of law is less than one-third of the book.[33] In legal practice, an appeal to the Koran has always been

---

the office went on as usual, except that people lowered their voices in deference to the candidate who was reciting in full voice. Over several months, I saw and heard at least twenty-five candidates, most of whom were thirty to thirty-five years old, though a few were in their twenties and some looked around fifty. Many of them had some marked physical disability, and perhaps five of those I saw were blind. The standards were high and the test a rigorous one. Most of the candidates I saw were visibly nervous, but the members of the committee were patient, friendly, and tried to put the candidates at their ease. As soon as a candidate completed the test, he left the room; the judges then wrote their individual decisions, discussed the composite rating they would give, and wrote their report. Of the candidates I saw examined, perhaps a quarter were successful.

No tourist, however short his stay in Egypt may have been, can have failed to hear Koran recitation. Radio and television devote programmes to it of sometimes considerable length. In television programmes the text which is recited is shown on the screen. Gramophone records with Koran recitation are also available.

[31] The *madhâhib*, "schools", of Islamic law do not always agree as to the category in which an act should be placed; moreover, the different schools know different "subdivisions and intermediate grades" between the categories mentioned.

[32] Not long ago Islamic law was frequently called "Koranic law", but at present this misleading appellation is not used by Western scholars who are genuinely interested in the Moslem world.

[33] *Hâshiyyat al-ʿAllâma al-Bannânî ʿalâ Sharh ... al-Mahallî ʿalâ Matn Gamʿ al-Gawâmiʿ li-l-Imâm ... ibn as-Subkî*, Cairo 1937, 2 vols., 432 & 440 pp.; Cf. *GAL* G II 89.

extremely rare.[34] Notwithstanding the limited value of the Koran for classical Islamic legal practice, the Koran does contain verses which do give concrete legislation on several topics, for instance the dissolution of marriages. Mohammed Abduh summarizes the history of the interpretation of these verses as follows:

> Some commentators of the Koran collected the verses that contain legal stipulations, and composed commentaries exclusively on these verses. The most famous of these commentators is Abû Bakr ibn al-ʿArabî. *Fiqh* got the better of many a commentator. They then concerned themselves with the interpretation of the legal verses more than with the interpretation of the rest of the verses of the Koran.[35]

How do the modern Egyptian Koran commentaries treat these "legal verses" (*âyât al-ahkâm*)? In the first place, the commentaries rarely go into the technicalities of the law. Even a Koran commentary written especially for the students of the faculty of law of the Azhar University [36] starts by discussing the legal verses in a philological way ("*lughatan*"), adds the Traditions connected with them, and mentions the occasions of the revelation (*asbâb an-nuzûl*). Then this commentary enumerates what legal topics are connected with each verse, but for the details it refers to the textbooks of the four schools of Islamic law (*kutub al-fiqh, kutub al-madhâhib*).

Secondly, the commentaries do not allude to the limited importance of Islamic law in the law of Egypt, although their authors are interested in this subject as can be demonstrated from other writings. For instance Mahmûd Shaltût wrote about the relation between the prescripts of the Koran and the terms of Egyptian law in his *Al-Islâm: ʿAqîda wa-Sharîʿa* (Islam: Creed and Law), but in his Koran commentary he is silent on this subject.[37] The same holds good for more traditional commentaries like those by Muhammad Farîd Wagdî, Sayyid Qutb, ʿAbd al-Karîm al-Khatîb or Ahmad

---

[34] Cf. J. Brugman, *De Betekenis van het Mohammedaanse Recht in het Hedendaagse Egypte*, Den Haag 1960.

[35] *Tafsîr al-Manâr*, i, 18. Abduh (and Ridâ) here refer to Abû Bakr b. al-ʿArabî (d. 1148), *Ahkâm al-Qurʾân*, a book still widely studied and often (re-)printed; Cp. *GAL* S I 663.

[36] Muhammad ʿAlî as-Sâyis, *Tafsîr Âyât al-Ahkâm*, 4 vols., Cairo (Kulliyyat as-Sharîʿa) 1953.

[37] Mahmûd Shaltût, *Al-Islâm: ʿAqîda wa-Sharîʿa*[3], Cairo 1966, 182 (on divorce); id., *Tafsîr al-Agzâʾ al-ʿAshara al-Ûlâ*[4], Cairo 1966. Reviews of this commentary in *Magallat al-Azhar*, xxxi, 1013 (March 1960), and xxxii, 112 (June 1960).

Mustafâ al-Marâghî: none of them thinks it appropiate (e.g. in their respective commentaries on Koran 2:228, in which rules for the dissolution of marriages are given) to mention the problem of the extent of the application of these rules. Most commentators seem to feel that this problem, important as it is, is better left untreated in a commentary on the Koran.[38] The complaint sometimes made by contemporary Moslems that Koran commentaries have become encyclopaedias in which law, philology, etc. are discussed extensively, but not "the Koran itself", no longer applies to the manner in which modern Egyptian Koran commentaries treat law, whether it be Islamic law or the law of Egypt.

Thirdly, the commentators treat Islamic law in an apologetic way. They greatly praise and extol it and tell us repeatedly in connection with the legal verses that no man-made law was ever better adapted to human nature than Islamic law, which is valid for all places and all times. The motive of the absolute fitness of Islamic law is complemented by stress on its relative merit. Especially in connection with what is nowadays regarded as cruel punishment (the chopping off of the right hand) or as socially undesirable (polygamy), it is stressed again and again that Islamic law is a great step forward compared with the laws and customs of the period of barbarism and ignorance which preceded the advent of Islam.

A question which occupies many students of contemporary Islam is whether "to exert oneself in the independent legal interpretation of the Koran and the Traditions from the Prophet", the so-called *Igtihâd*, is permitted to the modern Moslem. In the classical system, *Igtihâd* was only exercised by the venerable scholars of the past, and had disappeared after 1000 A.D. The question is usually put in the formula borrowed from the classical works on the "roots" of the law (*usûl al-fiqh*): "Is the gate of *Igtihâd* open?" Nowadays nearly all Moslems will answer this question in the affirmative. This agreement, however, is largely one of words: people agree that something called "*Igtihâd*" is permitted, but they do not agree as to what the term "*Igtihâd*" stands for. They disagree as to how far one may be independent of previous decisions in questions of Islamic law, and in what fields one should permit *Igtihâd*. (To permit *Igtihâd* in questions pertaining to the *ʿibâdât*, acts of devotion, is practically unheard of.)

---

[38] Cf., however, the commentary by Muhammad ʿAbd al-Munʿim Khafagî, published in Iraq: *Tafsîr al-Qurʾân al-Karîm*, Nagaf n.d., vl. vii, 85-105.

In their Koran commentary, Abduh and Ridâ frequently discuss
the problem of *Igtihâd*. The *Igtihâd* of previous generations is not
binding upon modern Moslems, they argue.[39] They even call it
ra'y,[40] this word originally meant "view", but in Islamic law it is
often used to designate a personal subjective view that is not based
on Koran and *Sunna*. *Igtihâd*, they argue, is a neccessary device of
Moslem law; to forbid it would make the divine law unadjustable
to changing circumstances, or, in Ridâ's words, "unfit for all
people at all times".[41] We should not use it "to add to religion in
accordance with our own tastes, but it is permitted to us in order
to discover what our welfare in this world is based upon".[42] Such a
remark, which is perhaps somewhat cryptic, means that re-interpretation of the Koran and re-consideration of its legal purport may
bring about a system of Islamic law that is better adjusted to
modern times and yet in accordance with the word of God. Those
prescripts of traditional Islamic law that are inapplicable in a
modern society, Abduh and Ridâ suggest, are "additions" to the
command of God, for which the jurists of the past are responsible.
Abduh and Ridâ attack those who oppose the exercise of *Igtihâd* by
contemporaries.[43] They realize that their attitude in this respect may
irritate many of their contemporaries.[44]

More than mere irritation was caused by Muhammad Abû Zayd's
ideas on *Igtihâd*. Abû Zayd, an Egyptian theologian from the town
of Damanhour, published a Koran commentary in 1930 which
caused some illuminating discussions on *Igtihâd*. Rashîd Ridâ
accused Abû Zayd of atheism, and at the same time of stealing
ideas from Abduh.[45] The Australian orientalist Arthur Jeffery
described Abû Zayd's Koran commentary as follows:

> The greater portion of each page is taken up by the text of the
> Qur'ān reproduced from a cheap lithograph commonly used by
> students in Cairo, and the margins to the side and bottom are
> devoted to the annotations of Sheikh Abū Zaid. These annotations
> are not extensive. Frequently they are nothing more than references
> to other passages in the Qur'ān which in the opinion of the author

[39] *Tafsîr al-Manâr*, vi, 194.
[40] ib., iv, 399.
[41] ib., vi, 420.
[42] ib., iii, 328.
[43] ib., ii, 356.
[44] ib., iv, 23.
[45] Arthur Jeffery, "The Suppressed Qur'ān Commentary of Muhammad
Abû Zaid", *Der Islam*, xx (1932), 301-8.

will shed some light on the verse under discussion. For the rest they are brief notes setting forth his idea as to how the verses should be interpreted. It is thus rather what we should call an annotated edition of the Qur'ān than a Commentary in the strict sense of the word. It is prefaced by 8 pages of Introduction in which he sets forth his principles of Interpretation.[46]

As Arthur Jeffery showed, the commentary is conceived in a spirit of a rationalism which does not differ much from Abduh's rationalist ideas. Nevertheless, the book raised a storm of protests. Abû Zayd himself claimed that the indignation which it evoked was due to political reasons. Jeffery denied this, but it is true that hidden allusions to the autocratic way in which monarchical Egypt was ruled under the régime of Prime Minister Sidqî and the King, could be read in a phrase like: "This verse teaches that Islam does not admit the rule of an individual"[47]—a perhaps unexpected comment on the use of a plural pronoun in Koran 4:(62)59 "O ye who have believed, obey... *those*[48] of you who have the command".[49]

The official report of the Azhar University[50] in which Abû Zayd's commentary is condemned, of course does not refer to political issues but to legal (and a few dogmatic) questions. On page 281 of his commentary, Abû Zayd teaches that deviations from the traditional prescripts of Islamic law are permitted if they aim at human welfare (*maslaha*) in the widest sense. This is virtually the same as what Abduh and Ridâ taught. Yet we read in the first chapter of the Azhar report on Abû Zayd and his commentary some violent remarks by the investigatory committee of Azhar scholars. Under the heading "The duty of obedience towards the Prophet" we are confronted with the following argument:

> ... to say that it is permitted to differ from the Prophet for the sake of what human welfare demands, leads to rejection of all prescripts of the noble law of Islam, on the pretext that human welfare requires not to carry out His command. How often do we hear people urging the rejection of our religion, saying that it is

---

[46] ib.

[47] Muhammad Abû Zayd, *Al-Hidâya wa-l-'Irfân fî Tafsîr al-Qur'ân bi-l-Qur'ân*, Cairo (Mustafâ al-Bâbî al-Halabî) 1349 A.H., *ad* Koran 4:(62)59.

[48] Italics added.

[49] Bell's translation. Abû Zayd's expression *hukûmat al-fard* "rule of an individual", is, of course, the exact Arabic translation of "monarchy".

[50] "*Taqrîr al-Lagna al-Azhariyya...*" in *Nûr al-Islâm*, ii, 163-206; 249-281. (Cairo 1350 A.H.).

a religion that fits a period past, a religion that became incompatible with our age . . . The prescripts of Islamic law have been established, so there is no place for personal views in it.[51]

Elsewhere, in his comment on Koran 2:(276)275 "Allah has forbidden . . . usury", Abû Zayd tries to reconcile Egyptian legal practice (which permits interest on money) and Islamic law (which does not) by defining *ribâ* (usury or interest) with the help of Koran 3:(125)130 "O ye who have believed, live not on usury doubled twice over, but act piously". Abû Zayd here explains that according to him the Koranic prohibition aims only at "exorbitant interest" (*ar-ribâ al-fâhish*) and not at a fair payment for the use of money borrowed. Here again the committee of experts becomes rather vehement and calls Abû Zayd's view "idiocy" (*sakhl*) and "adjustment to individual whims". The committee qualifies the opinions of Abû Zayd as "a call to *Igtihâd* that leaves the door wide open; there is much harm in it, clearly visible... We do not teach that *Igtihâd* is impossible or the exclusive privilege of a certain period of Islamic history, but we want to be moderate in it, avoiding exaggeration". To this committee, obviously, the term *Igtihâd* does not mean what it means to Abduh and Abû Zayd, but as the committee sees it, *Igtihâd* is only "the application of the revealed rules on cases on which no ruling has existed as yet." Other views they regard as "secret intrigues aiming at modification of the revealed law".[52]

The opposite view of *Igtihâd* can be found in the Koran commentary written by Mahmûd Shaltût—who was Rector of the Azhar University until his death in 1964.[53] When Shaltût writes about the sources of Islamic law, he avoids the classical terminology and does not use the appellation "roots" (*usûl*), but the modern word *masâdir* ("origins, sources"). In connection with Koran 4:)62)59 Shaltût writes: "*Igtihâd* is one of the three sources of the law. It has always been permitted... the first source of Islamic law is the Koran... the second, the custom of the Prophet, whether it be his words or his acts." In the same passage Shaltût calls the third source *ra'y*—the term reserved in the classical terminology for "a personal subjective view that is not based on Koran and

[51] ib., 176.
[52] ib., 170.
[53] On Shaltût in general: Ahmad Hasan az-Zayyât, "Al-Imâm al-Akbar as-Shaykh Mahmûd as-Shaltût," in *Magallat al-Azhar*, xxxv, 641 (January 1964).

Sunna".[54] Ridâ used this term to discredit the *Igtihâd* of previous generations,[55] but in Shaltût's terminology this much-used and laden term serves as the equivalent of the classical term *Igtihâd*. The idea that the sources of Islamic law are three in number (Koran, *Sunna* and *Ra'y* or *Igtihâd*), however, is not only found in Shaltût's Koran commentary, but also in his systematic résumé *Al-Islâm*: *'Aqîda wa-Sharî'a* [56] (Islam: Creed and Law).[57]

In the latter work Shaltût first discusses the creed in about seventy pages, then the law in about four hundred pages. He concludes this work with a chapter of nearly a hundred pages on the "sources" of the law. According to Shaltût these are Koran, *Sunna* and *Ra'y*. It is consequently more or less surprising that a reviewer of the book writes in the journal of the Azhar University:[58] "The book ends with an essay on the sources of Islamic law, namely the Koran, the *Sunna*, *Qiyâs* [analogy], and *Igmâ'* [agreement]", because the book clearly does not end with these classical four roots, but with a "progressive", and possibly heretical theory, which is loosely connected with Koran 4:(62)59 "O ye who have believed, obey Allah and obey the messenger..." Shaltût's views on the sources of Islamic law, and his insistence on the legitimacy of *Igtihâd*, however, bring him seldom, if ever, into conflict with the traditional terms, regulations and precepts of Islamic law, as is shown by his "orthoprax" *fatwas* [59] (counsels in matters of Islamic law) and his other articles.[60] This carefulness on his part earned for him the praise of many contemporaries, for instance of Ahmad Hasan az-Zayyât, also a conservative reformer, who wrote in an article on Shaltût in the journal of the Azhar:[61]

> Shaltût had no need for heretical *Igtihâd* (Ar.: *Igtihâd mubtadi'*) but his *Igtihâd* was of another kind: it was the *Igtihâd* of selecting

[54] Mahmûd Shaltût, *Tafsîr . . .*, 208.
[55] *Tafsîr al-Manâr*, iv, 399.
[56] Mahmûd Shaltût, *Al-Islâm*: *'Aqîda wa-Sharî'a*, 477 ff.; 552 ff. (*ra'y*); id., *Min Hudâ al-Qur'ân*, 7 (*Igtihâd*).
[57] The title of this important book briefly states the program of the "conservative reformers", as opposed to the program of the "conservative extremists", the Moslem Brothers, whose program ran: *Al-Islâm*: *Dîn wa-Dawla*, "Islam: Religion and State". Cp. e.g. *Zâd al-Khatîb*, Cairo (Wizârat al-Awqâf) 1964, 66: a *Khutba* under the title *Al-Islâm*: *'Aqîda wa-Sharî'a*.
[58] 'Abd al-Galîl Shalabî, "Min Mu'allafât al-Imâm ar-Râhil", in: *Magallat al-Azhar*, xxxv, 711a (January 1964).
[59] Mahmûd Shaltût, *Al-Fatâwâ*[3], Cairo 1966.
[60] id., *Min Tawgîhât al-Islâm*[3], Cairo 1966.
[61] *Magallat al-Azhar*, xxxv, 643a.

the suitable view and of giving due preponderance to the right decision.

In the beginning of the nineteenth century the official doctrine on *Igtihâd* was still comparatively simple. In the Shâfi'î handbook of Islamic law by the popular jurist Al-Bâgûrî (d. 1860) we read that the gate of *Igtihâd* was closed at the end of the third century A.H.[62] In the twentieth century, however, the doctrine lost its attractive simplicity. Perhaps the most illuminating statement about it was made by Dr. I. M. as-Sharqâwî, who wrote: "The modern Koran commentators have opened the gate of *the debate around* the *Igtihâd*..."[63]

It should be borne in mind, however, that *Igtihâd* is not the real motor of change in Islamic law, even if the theory of the Moslem jurists would so prescribe. *Igtihâd* serves to justify in retrospective the changes that are brought about by outside forces, first of all Western influence on ideas in the Arab and Moslem world on what is socially desirable. This is particularly clear in the modern treatment of what the Koran has to say about marriage and polygamy. Polygamy is traditionally linked with Koran 4:(3)3 "...marry such of the women as seem good to you, double or treble or four-fold—but if you fear that ye may not be capable of dealing with them evenly, then one..."[64]

In the older commentaries the problem in the exegesis of this verse is not whether the Koran does indeed permit polygamy. They sometimes even discuss whether the formula used in this verse implies unlimited polygamy, or whether it limits the number of legal wives to four.[65] The idea that polygamy is a debatable practice does not occur in commentaries before the nineteenth century. Even a comparatively recent commentary (that by Al-Qâsimî, a Syrian who worked at the end of the nineteenth century) tells us about the condition set to polygamy in Koran 4:3 "if you fear that you may not be capable of dealing with them evenly": "Scholars agree that the condition set in this verse has no meaning (*lâ mafhûm*

---

[62] Th. W. Juynboll, *Handleiding tot de Kennis van de Mohammedaansche Wet volgens de leer der Sjâfi'itische School*, Leiden 1930; *Hâshiyyat al-Bâgûrî 'alâ Matn Ibn Qâsim al-Ghazzî ... 'alâ Matn ... Abî Shugâ'*, Cairo ('Îsâ al-Bâbî al-Halabî) n.d., 19.

[63] I. Muhammad as-Sharqâwî, *Ittigâhât at-Tafsîr fî Misr fî-l-'Asr al-Hadîth*, Cairo 1972.

[64] Bell's translation.

[65] Cf. the Koran commentary of Fakhr ad-Dîn ar-Râzî.

lahú)".[66] However, some modern Moslems argue that since no man can be impartial between several women, the passage "...if you fear..." virtually makes polygamy impossible.[67]

In this respect, the most radical attitude is taken by 'Abd al-'Azîz Fahmî,[68] who concludes that polygamy is explicitly forbidden by the Koran.[69] His textual argument is taken from the same sura, from Koran 4:(128)129 "Ye will not be capable of dealing evenly among women, even though you try". In conjunction with Koran 4:3 "if you fear that ye may not be capable of dealing with them evenly, then one..." this looks impressive indeed. Nevertheless, although Fahmî bases himself exclusively on the text of the Koran and on (complicated) deductions from Islamic history, in the polemics against him he is accused of being under heavy Western influence. In an almost sarcastic article [70] about him, a certain Ahmad Muhammad Gamâl reminds the reader that 'Abd al-'Azîz Fahmî also put forward a strange view (*ra'y 'agîb*) on the necessity of replacing the Arabic alphabet by Latin characters [71] — obviously Gamâl says so in order to discredit Fahmî in the eyes of the public, and to expose him as a Westernizer. Gamâl, a witty polemist, then calls Fahmî's view on polygamy "stranger yet (*a'gab*)". Surprisingly enough, he does not attack Fahmî with exegetical arguments alone, but also with arguments based on what Gamâl holds to be socially desirable. A society in which polygamy is allowed is more just than a society in which it is forbidden, so he argues, because it is possible to imagine situations that are better solved by permitting the husband to take a second wife, than by divorce. Polygamy is in no way morally inferior to monogamy, according to Ahmad Muhammad Gamâl, if only because of the hypocrisy monogamy may lead to.

Rashîd Ridâ, who also felt the need to defend [72] Islam against

---

[66] Al-Qâsimî, *Mahâsin at-Ta'wîl*, p. 1107.

[67] Cf. the remark made by W. M. Watt, *Companion to the Qur'ân*, 62; J. Brugman, *De Betekenis van het Mohammedaanse Recht in het Hedendaagse Egypte*, 82; Qâsim Amîn, *Tahrîr al-Mar'a*, Cairo 1899, 128.

[68] Egyptian Minister of Justice from 13th March to 5th September 1925, cp. M. Colombe, *L'évolution de l'Egypte*, 26 & 330.

[69] 'Abd al-'Azîz Fahmî, *Hâdhih Hayâtî*, Cairo n.d. (Kitâb al-Hilâl), 166 ff. This article was originally published in the periodical *Al-Mugtama' al-Gadîd*.

[70] Ahmad Muhammad Gamâl, *Ma'a al-Mufassirîn*, 30 ff.

[71] 'Abd al-'Azîz Fahmî, *Al-Hurûf al-Lâtiniyya li-Kitâbat al-'Arabiyya*, Cairo 1946.

[72] A neat summary of the arguments of the apologists on polygamy may

Western criticism on the point of polygamy, furthermore quotes in the Manar commentary long passages from rather obscure Western authors who did not fully disapprove of polygamy or who supplied him with arguments against the hypocrisy of the Christian Western world that forbade polygamy, but silently allowed the secret practising of adultery. In this way he endeavours to convince the readers of the Manar commentary that the West and its missionaries lack the moral right to blame Islam for permitting polygamy. The nicest argument in the polygamy debate is put forward by ʿAbbâs Mahmûd al-ʿAqqâd. Al-ʿAqqâd argues that the West has no right to criticize Moslems for practising polygamy, and that Christianity can in no way claim credit for forbidding polygamy, since the Christian prohibition of polygamous marriages does not spring from the high standards of Christian morality but, on the contrary, is a result of the low esteem in which women were held by early Christianity: women were regarded as an evil of which man should have as little as possible.[73]

As appears from the Koran commentaries, the general modernist opinion on polygamy since the beginning of the twentieth century is that polygamy is allowed if the circumstances make other solutions to the marital problems of the husband impossible or unjust to one of the parties involved. This change of view, from general permission of polygamy to the present restriction of it as a *darûra nâdira*, a rare necessity, is accompanied by a re-interpretation of certain passages from the Koran. Nevertheless, as at least one Egyptian observer agrees, it is not brought about by the Koran or Koran interpretation but by Western influence on Egyptian social values.[74]

That it is indeed Western influence and not the Koran itself, or its interpreters, that have caused changes of opinion like the change that took place concerning polygamy, can be demonstrated by the fact that the most heard Koranic argument which is employed to justify the modification of a traditional precept of Islamic law, is not—as in the case of polygamy—new emphasis on a verse from the Koran or a fresh interpretation of it or a new combination

---

be found in J. Brugman, *De Betekenis van het Mohammedaanse Recht in het Hedendaagse Egypte*, 143 ff.

[73] ʿAbbâs Mahmûd al-ʿAqqâd, *Al-Falsafa al-Qurʾâniyya*, Cairo 1962, p. 55.

[74] Cf. I. M. as-Sharqâwî, o.c., 217-223. Orthodox conservatives still attach great value to the legitimacy of polygamy.

of verses, but the argument that the Koran is silent on the matter. This argument is put forward by ʿAlî ʿAbd ar-Râziq when he suggests that a Caliphate which has worldly powers is not a necessary part of Moslem religion; [75] by Rashîd Ridâ when he seeks to remove from Moslem penal law the death penalty for apostasy from Islam,[76] and by Qâsim Amîn when he wants to abolish the seclusion and veiling of women.[77] It is difficult to see how the Koran by being silent could influence people to adopt a set of new opinions. Taking into consideration the similarity to Western views on Papal powers, religious freedom and the emancipation of women, there remains little reason to doubt that it was indeed Western influence which was responsible for these changes of opinion that have taken place in the Egyptian Moslem milieu. Nevertheless, the extent of the domination of the Koran becomes clear when we take notice of the fact that every Western idea to which Egyptian Moslems have attached value, has had to be harmonized with the Koran.[78]

Some conservative Moslems do not approve of these and similar attempts to harmonize Western ideas with the Koran and thus introduce them into the Moslem world. For instance, when certain reformers want to try to make use of exegesis in order to mitigate the punishment for theft which is prescribed by the Koran (the chopping off of the hand of the thief), a conservative Moslem charges the modernist reformers with "accusing Islamic law of cruelty".[79] The discussion between conservatives and reformers in such cases appears to be about the Koran and its correct interpretation, but in reality it is the extent to which parties approve of Western ideas that is under discussion.

Muhammad Kâmil Husayn, with a half-serious joke, makes this abundantly clear.[80] Capitalism, he sneers, can be made Islamic by pointing to Koran 2:(279)279 "ye retain your capital, no wrong being done on either side", and dictatorship by pointing to Koran 4:(62)59 "obey those of you who have the command", and the parliamentary system by Koran 42:(36)38 "Their affair being a counsel amongst them".

---

[75] A. Hourani, *Arabic Thought in the Liberal Age*, 185.
[76] ib., 237.
[77] ib., 165.
[78] Cf. M. H. Kerr, *Islamic Reform*, 209.
[79] Ramzî Naʿnâʿa, *Bidaʿ at-Tafâsîr*, Amman 1970, 83.
[80] Muhammad Kâmil Husayn, *Ad-Dhikr al-Hakîm*, 187.

CONCLUSION

It is difficult to draw comparisons between the exegesis of the Koran and the exegesis of the Bible for two reasons. Firstly, the position of the Koran within Islam differs considerably from the position of the Bible within Christianity, since Moslems consider the Koran to be the uncreated Word of God almost in the way in which Christians consider Jesus of Nazareth to be the Son of God. Secondly, in Judaism and Christianity the community of believers itself decided in a gradual process which texts would or would not be included in the canon of the Holy Scripture. It was not until the canon was closed that there was a large-scale need for an interpretation of the holy texts. On the other hand, when the Prophet Mohammed died in 632 A.D., the Moslem community was confronted with an immediate need to explain and apply the holy texts which they had received through Mohammed. After his death there was, quite obviously, no hope of receiving "supplementary" revelations. It was for this reason that, at short notice, the believers were faced with the task of providing interpretations and applications of the extant material. This might explain why, from the very beginning, the exegesis of the Koran seemed somewhat artificial.

In orientalist circles, there has always been a great amount of interest in the Moslem exegesis of the Koran. The large number of Koran commentaries which were published in Egypt since the beginning of the century and to which the Western works on Koran exegesis and its history (the most important being those by I. Goldziher, J. Jomier and J. M. S. Baljon) do not refer, might warrant our granting this topic closer attention.

The contents of the modern Egyptian commentaries are made up of remarks on the philology of the Koran; remarks on the Koran and natural history; and remarks on the Koran and the day-to-day affairs of the Moslems in this world. It might be said that there are three aspects to the modern Egyptian Koran commentaries: a natural history aspect, a philological aspect and a practical aspect. The contents of each commentary are more or less heterogeneous. It would, therefore, not be quite accurate to speak of three "tendencies" in modern Koran exegesis, certainly not if this were taken to mean that the mass of commentaries could be divided into three groups in accordance with these three tendencies.

Perhaps it is inevitable that a commentary on a holy text should have these three aspects: the "literal" meaning of the text (philological exegesis), the significance of the text with respect to man's actions (practical exegesis), and the significance of the text with respect to man's knowledge ("scientific" exegesis, *tafsîr 'ilmî*). It might be possible to analyze the older commentaries in a similar manner. At any rate, the Koran commentaries which have been produced since the time of Mohammed Abduh (1848/9-1905) do possess these three aspects.

There is no Great Wall of China between the old and the new commentaries. It is often difficult to understand one without the other. Nowadays, Egyptians who decide to devote their attention to Koran exegesis study both groups of commentaries side by side. The most important difference between the two groups seems to be that the "classical" commentaries were written in an era when the people who could read were almost solely those who had received a theological training, whereas the modern commentaries (often explicitly) address a public who have learned to read and write outside the mosque. Nevertheless, form and contents of modern commentaries are often surprisingly traditional.

It is remarkable that Moslems working on "scientific" exegesis do make use of the Western natural sciences, be it on a level where it might be more accurate to speak of elementary "natural history". In Judaism and Christianity, on the other hand, the text of the Holy Scripture has often been utilized to find out historical truths: certain Jews and Christians were often of the opinion that the date of the hoped-for fall of an inimical empire could be derived from close scrutiny of the Scriptures. This kind of "historical" exegesis is almost unknown to the Moslems.

Moslem philological exegesis can never be based on the *e mente auctoris* principle which prevails in certain Christian circles, because Moslems believe that God is the "author" of the Koran. However, the *e mente auctoris* principle is usually employed in a negative way: a certain interpretation which is unwelcome for one reason or another, is rejected because, for example, the Evangelist Luke, when noting down the text of the Gospel, could not have had it in mind. The fact that man is not in a position to judge what an omniscient God has or has not in mind, makes the *e mente auctoris* principle impractible as a "negative" exegetical rule for Moslem Koran interpreters. However, there is an equivalent to this principle which modern Koran commentators do use: many of them are of the opinion that the Koran must be understood primarily as the first Moslems in Mecca and Medina understood it, and that an interpretation which does not fit in with this milieu is not legitimate.

Lastly, it is noteworthy that the Moslem philological Koran exegesis exhibits a certain degree of stratification. Its first "layer", the study of the exact meaning of the individual words of the Koran, already existed at the time of Ibn 'Abbâs (seventh century A.D.); the second layer, the study of the syntax of the Koran, starting with the work of Abû 'Ubayda (ninth century A.D.), culminated in the work of Az-Zamakhsharî (twelfth century A.D.). Little from these layers has been lost. In the most recent commentaries, there are clear traces of the work of Ibn 'Abbâs, Abû 'Ubayda and Az-Zamakhsharî.

The practical exegesis of the Koran is still concerned with the entire life of the Moslems. Not only devotional questions like fasting, but also mundane matters like penal law and discord in the Moslem community are touched upon. While reading the exegetical discussions on such topics one has to take into account that as far as the discussion does not consist of edifying generalities, it often only makes the pretence of being concerned with the Koran and its proper interpretation. Often the true subject of the debate is the degree to which Western influence on the secular and religious aspects of life should be tolerated.

BIBLIOGRAPHY

Adams, C. C., *Islam and Modernism in Egypt*, New York 1968 [2]

Ahlwardt, W., *Verzeichnis der arabischen Handschriften der Königlichen Bibliothek in Berlin*, Berlin 1887-99.

Ahmad, A. M., *Die Auseinandersetzungen zwischen al-Azhar und der modernistischen Bewegung in Ägypten*, Hamburg 1963.

Ahmed, J. M., *The Intellectual Origins of Egyptian Nationalism*, London 1968.

Baljon, J. M. S., *Modern Muslim Koran Interpretation (1880-1960)*, Leiden 1961.

Beeston, A. F. L., *Written Arabic*, Cambridge 1968.

——, *Baidâwî's commentary on Sûrah 12 of the Qurʾân*, Oxford 1963.

Bell, Richard, *The Qurʾân Translated*, 2 vols., Edinburgh 1937.

Berger, M., *Islam in Egypt Today, Social and Political Aspects of Popular Religion*, Cambridge 1970.

Berkes, N., *The Development of Secularism in Turkey*, Montreal 1964.

Blachère, R., *Le problème de Mahomet*, Paris 1952.

——, *Introduction au Coran*, Paris 1959[2].

——, *Le Coran (al-Qorʾân) traduit de l'arabe*, Paris 1957.

Brockelmann, Carl, *Geschichte der arabischen Litteratur*, 5 vols., Leiden 1937-1949[2].

Brugman, J., *De Betekenis van het Mohammedaanse Recht in het Hedendaagse Egypte*, Den Haag 1960.

Colombe, M., *L'Evolution de l'Egypte 1924-1950*, Paris 1951.

Coulson, N. J., *A History of Islamic Law*, Edinburgh 1964.

Cragg, K., *Counsels in Contemporary Islam*, Edinburgh 1965.

Doeve, J. W., *Jewish Hermeneutics in the Synoptic Gospels and Acts*, Assen 1953.

Empson, William, *Seven Types of Ambiguity*, Harmondsworth (Pelican) 1973 [3].

The Encyclopaedia of Islam, Leiden 1960 [2]→

Fluegel, G., *Corani Textus Arabicus*, Leipzig 1883[3].

Forster, E. M., *Aspects of the Novel*, Harmondsworth (Penguin) 1971.

Gardet, L. et M.-M. Anawati, *Introduction à la théologie musulmane*, Paris 1948.

Gätje, H., *Koran und Koranexegese*, Zürich 1971.

Gibb, H. A. R., *Modern Trends in Islam*, Chicago 1950.

Gibb, H. A. R. and J. H. Kramers, *Shorter Encyclopaedia of Islam*, Leiden 1961.

Goldziher, I., *Die Zâhiriten*, Leipzig 1884.

——, *Die Richtungen der Islamischen Koranauslegung*, Leiden 1920.

Graf, L. I., *Al-Shâfiʿî's Verhandeling over de ,,Wortelen'' van den Fikh*, Amsterdam 1934.

Hourani, A., *Arabic Thought in the Liberal Age 1798-1939*, London 1970.

Jansen, J. J. G., " "I suspect that my friend Abduh (. . .) was in reality an Agnostic" ", in P. W. Pestman, ed., *Acta Orientalia Neerlandica*, Leiden 1971.

Jeffery, A., "The Suppressed Qurʾân Commentary of Muhammad Abû Zaid", *Der Islam*, xx (1932), 301-8.

——, *The Qurʾân as Scripture*, New York 1952.

Jomier, J., *Le commentaire coranique du Manâr*, Paris 1954.
——, "Quelques position actuelles de l'exégèse coranique en Egypte révélées par une polémique récente (1947-1951)", *MIDEO* 1 (1954), 39-72.
——, "Le Cheikh Tantâwî Jawharî (1862-1940) et son commentaire du Coran", *MIDEO* 5 (1958), 115-174.
—— & P. Caspar, "L'exégèse scientifique du Coran d'après le Cheikh Amîn al-Khûlî", *MIDEO* 4 (1957), 269-280.
Juynboll, G. H. A., *The Authenticity of the Tradition Literature, Discussions in Modern Egypt*, Leiden 1969.
Juynboll, Th. W., *Handleiding tot de Kennis van de Mohammedaansche Wet volgens de leer der Sjâfiʾitische School*, Leiden 1930.
Keddie, N. R., *Sayyid Jamâl ad-Dîn "al-Afghânî", a Political Biography*, Berkeley 1972.
Kedourie, E., *Afghani and ʿAbduh, an Essay on Religious Unbelief and Political Activism in Modern Islam*, London 1966.
Kerr, M. H., *Islamic Reform, the Political and Legal Theories of Muhammad ʾAbduh and Rashîd Ridâ*, Berkeley 1966.
Kramers, J. H., *De Koran uit het Arabisch vertaald*, Amsterdam 1956.
Lyall, Ch. J., *A Commentary on Ten Ancient Arabic Poems . . . by At-Tibrîzî*, Calcutta 1894.
Landau, J. M., *Parliaments and Parties in Egypt*, Tel-Aviv 1953.
MacDonald, D. B., *Development of Muslim Theology, Jurisprudence and Constitutional Theory*, Lahore 1903.
Mensing, J. P. M., *De Bepaalde Straffen in het Hanbalietische Recht*, Leiden 1936.
Meursinge, A., ed., *Sojutii Librum de Interpretibus Korani*, Leiden 1839.
Miskotte, H. H., *Sensus Spiritualis*, Nijkerk 1966.
Mitchell, R. P., *The Society of the Muslim Brothers*, London 1969.
Mubârak, Zaki, *La prose arabe au IVe siècle de l'Hégire*, Paris 1931.
Nöldeke, Th., —— F. Schwally, et al., *Geschichte des Qorâns*, 3 vols., Leipzig 1909².
Nussayr, A. I., *Arabic Books Published in . . . Egypt between 1926 & 1940*, Cairo 1969.
Pellat, Ch., *Langue et littérature arabes*, Paris 1952.
Russell, B., *Religion and Science*, London [1935].
Safran, N., *Egypt in Search of Political Community*, Cambridge Mass. 1961.
Schacht, J., *An Introduction to Islamic Law*, Oxford 1964.
——, *The Origins of Muhammadan Jurisprudence*, Oxford 1967.
Sezgin, Fuat, *Geschichte des Arabischen Schrifttums*, Band I, Leiden (Brill) 1967.
Smith, W. C., *Modern Islam in India*, London 1946.
——, *Islam in Modern History*, Princeton 1957.
Sontag, Susan, *Against Interpretation*, New York 1961.
Szasz, Th. S., *The Manufacture of Madness*, New York (Paladin) 1972.
——, *The Myth of Mental Illness*, New York (Paladin) 1972.
Watt, W. M., *Muhammad at Medina*, Oxford 1956.
——, *Muhammad at Mecca*, Oxford 1960.
——, *Companion to the Qurʾân, based on the Arberry Translation*, London 1967.
——, *Bell's Introduction to the Qurʾân*, Edinburgh 1970.
Wellek, R., and A. Warren, *Theory of Literature*, Harmondsworth 1963³.
Wellhausen, J., *Reste Arabischen Heidentums*, Berlin 1897².
Wensinck, A. J., *A Handbook of Early Muhammadan Tradition*, Leiden 1971².

——, *The Muslim Creed*, London 1932.
White, A. D., *A History of the Warfare of Science with Theology in Christendom*, Abridged with a preface and epilogue by Bruce Mazlish, New York 1965.
Wielandt, R., *Offenbarung und Geschichte im Denken moderner Muslime*, Wiesbaden 1971.
Wilkinson, J., *Interpretation and Community*, London 1963.
Wright, W., *A Grammar of the Arabic Language*, Cambridge 1896-1898[3].
Zwaan, J. de, *Inleiding tot het Nieuwe Testament*, Haarlem 1948[2].

* *
*

ʿAbbâs al-Gamal, *Âyat al-Birr min Âyât al-Qurʾân al-ʿAzîm*, Matb. Lagnat at-Taʾlîf wa-t-Targama wa-n-Nashr, Cairo 1371/1952.
ʿAbbâs Mahmûd al-ʿAqqâd, "Tafsîr al-Ustâdh al-Imâm", in *Magallat al-Azhar*, XXXV, 389 (November 1963).
——, *Al-Falsafa al-Qurʾâniyya*, Dâr al-Hillâl, Cairo [1966].
——, *Sâʿât bayn al-Kutub*, Makt. an-Nahda al-Misriyya, Cairo 1968[4].
——, *Al-Insân fî-l-Qurʾân al-Karîm*, Dâr al-Hilâl, Cairo n.d.
——, *Al-Marʾa fî-l-Qurʾân*, Dâr al-Hilâl, Cairo n.d.
ʿAbd al-ʿAzîm Ahmad al-Ghubâshî, *Taʾrîkh at-Tafsîr wa-Manâhig al-Mufassirîn*, Dâr at-Tibâʿa al-Muhammadiyya, Cairo 1971.
ʿAbd al-ʿAzîm Maʿânî & Ahmad Ghandûr, *Ahkâm min al-Qurʾân wa-s-Sunna*, ad-Dâr al-Maʿârif, Cairo 1965.
ʿAbd al-ʿAzîz Fahmî, *Hâdhih Hayâtî*, Dâr al-Hilâl, Cairo 1963.
ʿAbd al-ʿAzîz Ismâʿîl, *Al-Islâm wa-t-Tibb al-Hadîth*, Matb. al-Iʿtimâd, Cairo 1938.
ʿAbd al-Fattâh, v. Ibrâhîm ʿAzzûr.
ʿAbd al-Fattâh Khalîfa, *Tafsîr Sûrat al-Hâqqa*, Magallat al-Islâm, Cairo n.d.
ʿAbd al-Galîl ʿÎsâ, *Al-Mushaf al-Muyassar*, Dâr as-Shurûq, Cairo 1389/1969[4].
ʿAbd al-Hamîd Kuhayl Dâwud, *Yûsuf, ʿalayh as-Salâm, Nazarât fî-t-Tafsîr*, Ad-Dâr al-Qawmiyya, Cairo 1966.
ʿAbd al-Karîm al-Khatîb, *Iʿgâz al-Qurʾân*, 2 vols., Dâr al-Fikr al-ʿArabî, Cairo 1964.
——, *At-Tafsîr al-Qurʾân li-l-Qurʾân*, 16 vols., Dâr al-Fikr al-ʿArabî, Cairo 1967-197 .
ʿAbd al-Latîf as-Subkî, *Nafahât al-Qurʾân*, 2 vols., Al-Maglis al-Aʿlâ li-s-Shuʾûn al-Islâmiyya, Cairo 1964.
ʿAbd al-Mutaʿâl as-Saʿîdî, *Igtihâd Gadîd fî Âyat "wa-ʿalâ-lladhîn yutîqûnah fidya"*, Matb. al-ʿtimâd, Cairo 1374/1955.
——, *Dirâsât Qurʾâniyya*, Dâr al-Fikr al-ʿArabî, Cairo 1378/1959.
——, *Al-Azhar wa-Kitâb Dirâsât Qurʾâniyya*, Dâr at-Thaqâfa li-t-Tibâʿa, Cairo 1383/1964.
——, *An-Nazm al-Fannî fî-l-Qurʾân*, Makt. al-Âdâb, Cairo n.d.
ʿAbd al-Qâdir Ahmad ʿAtâ, *At-Tafsîr as-Sûfî li-l-Qurʾân (Dirâsa wa-Tahqîq li-Kitâb Iʿgâz al-Bayân fî Taʾwîl Umm al-Qurʾân li-Abî al-Maʿâlî .. al-Qûnawî)*, Dâr al-Kutub al-Hadîtha, Cairo 1969.
ʿAbd al-Qâdir al-Maghribî, *al-Qurʾân al-Karîm: Guzʾ Tabârak*, as-Shaʿb, Cairo 1968.
——, *ʿAlâ Hâmish at-Tafsîr*, Makt. al-Âdâb, Cairo n.d.
ʿAbd ar-Rahîm Fawda, *Min Maʿânî al-Qurʾân*, Dâr al-Kitâb al-ʿArabî, Cairo n.d.

ʿAbd ar-Rahmân al-Bannâ', *Min Maʿânî al-Qur'ân, Tafsîr Sûrat al-Hugarât*, Cairo n.d. [1960/1].

ʿAbd ar-Rahmân al-Bannânî, *Hâshiyat al-Allâma al-Bannânî ʿalâ Sharh al-Galâl . . . al-Mahallî ʿalâ Matn Gamʿ al-Gawâmiʿ li-l-Imâm Tâg ad-Dîn ʿAbd al-Wahhâb b. as-Subkî*, Mustafâ al-Bâbî al-Halabî, Cairo 1938.

ʿAbd ar-Rahmân Shâhîn, *Iʿgâz al-Qur'ân wa-l-Iktishâfât al-Hadîtha*, Matb. al-Ismâʿiliyya al-Kubrâ, n.p. 1369/1950[3].

ʿAbd ar-Razzâq Nawfal, *Allâh wa-l-ʿIlm al-Hadîth*, Makt. Misr, Cairo 1376/1957.

ʿAbd as-Sabûr Shânîn, *Ta'rîkh al-Qur'ân*, Dâr al-Qalam, Cairo 1966.

ʿAbdallâh Mahmûd Shihâta, *Manhag al-Imâm Muhammad ʿAbduh fî Tafsîr al-Qur'ân al-Karîm*, Cairo 1963.

ʿAbdallâh Muhammad Ahmad Muhammad ʿUlaysh, *Îdâh Ibdâʿ Hikmat al-Hakîm fî Bayân Bismillâh ar-Rahmân ar-Rahîm*, Mustafâ al-Babî al-Halabî, Cairo 1373/1954.

ʿAbduh, v. Muhammad ʿAbduh.

Abd al-Wahhâb Hamûda, "At-Tafsîr al-ʿIlmî li-l-Qur'ân", *Magallat al-Azhar* xxx (1958) 279.

——, *Al-Qur'ân wa-ʿIlm an-Nafs*, Cairo 1962.

Abû ʿAbdallâh az-Zangânî, *Ta'rîkh al-Qur'ân*, Makt. as-Sadr, Tehrân 1387.

Abû al-Fadl ʿAbdallâh Muhammad as-Sadîq al-Ghumârî, *Bidaʿ at-Tafâsîr*, Makt. al-Qâhira, Cairo 1965.

Abû ʿUbayda, *Magâz al-Qur'ân*, Ed. F. Sezgin, 2 vols., Makt. al-Khângî, Cairo 1954-1962.

Abû Zayd, v. Muhammad Abû Zayd.

Al-Abyârî, v. Ibrâhîm al-Abyârî.

Ahmad Ahmad Badawî, *Min Balâghat al-Qur'ân*, Makt. Nahdat Misr, Cairo n.d.[3].

Ahmad Khalîl, *Nash'at at-Tafsîr fî-l-Kutub al-Muqaddasa wa-l-Qur'ân*, Al-Wakâla as-Sharqiyya li-t-Thaqâfa, Alexandria 1373/1954.

Ahmad Khalîl, *Dirâsât fî-l-Qur'ân*, Dâr al-Maʿârif, Cairo 1971.

Ahmad Khalîl, *Hukm al-Mathânî, Tafsîr li-l-Qur'ân al-Karîm, Gamʿ al-ʿUlûm ad-Dîniyya wa-s-Sûfiyya wa-l-ʿAsriyya*, Matb. al-Kîlânî as-Saghîr, Cairo 1968.

Ahmad Muhammad Gamâl, *Maʿa al-Mufassirîn wa-l-Kitâb*, Dâr al-Kitâb al-ʿArabî, Cairo n.d.

Ahmad Muhammad al-Hûfî, *At-Tabarî*, Aʿlâm al-ʿArab 13, Cairo 1962.

Ahmad Mustafâ al-Marâghî, *Mudhakkirat at-Tafsîr*, Cairo 1937.

——, *Tafsîr al-Marâghî*, 30 vols., Mustafa al-Bâbî al-Halabî, Cairo 1962[3].

Ahmad as-Sharabâsî, *Qissat at-Tafsîr*, Dâr al-Qalam, Cairo 1962.

——, *Rashîd Ridâ, Sâhib al-Manâr, ʿAsruh wa-Hayâtuh wa-Masâdir Thaqâfatih*, Al-Maglis al-Aʿlâ li-s-Shu'ûn al-Islâmiyya, Cairo 1970.

ʿÂ'isha ʿAbd ar-Rahmân, *At-Tafsîr al-Bayânî li-l-Qur'ân al-Karîm*, 2 vols., Dâr al-Maʿârif, Cairo 1966[2], 1969[1].

——, *Maqâl fî-l-Insân*, Dâr al-Maʿârif, Cairo 1969.

——, *Al-Qur'ân wa-t-Tafsîr al-ʿAsrî*, Iqra' 335, Cairo 1970.

——, *Al-Iʿgâz al-Bayânî li-l-Qur'ân wa-Masâ'il Ibn al-Azraq*, Dar al-Maʿârif, Cairo 1971.

Amîn, v. ʿUthmân Amîn.

Amîn al-Khûlî, *At-Tafsîr, Maʿâlim Hayâtih-Manhaguh al-Yawm*, Cairo 1944.

——, *Min hudâ al-Qur'ân, al-Qâda . . . ar-Rusul*, Dâr al-Maʿrifa, Cairo 1959.

——, *Min Hudâ al-Qur'ân, Fî Ramadân*, Dâr al-Maʿrifa, Cairo n.d.

——, *Min Hudâ al-Qur'ân, Fî Amwâlhim, Mithâliyya, Lâ Madhhabiyya*, Dâr al-Ma'rifa, Cairo n.d.

——, *Manâhig Tagdîd fî-n-Nahw wa-l-Balâgha wa-t-Tafsîr wa-l-Adab*, Dâr al-Ma'rifa, Cairo 1961. (Collection of previously published articles).

Anwar al-Gundî, *Tarâgim al-A'lâm al-Mu'âsirîn fî-l-'Âlam al-Islâmî*, Makt. al-Anglû al-Misriyya, Cairo 1970.

——, *Ma'âlim al-Fikr al-'Arabî al-Mu'âsir*, Matb. ar-Risâla, Cairo n.d.

——, *Al-Muhâfaza wa-t-Tagdîd fî-n-Nathr al-'Arabî al-Mu'âsir fî Mî'at 'Âmm*, Matb. ar-Risâla, Cairo n.d.

Al-'Aqqâd, v. 'Abbâs Mahmûd al-'Aqqâd.

b. 'Âshûr, v. Muhammad al-Fâdil b. 'Âshûr, & Muhammad at-Tâhir b. 'Âshûr.

Al-Baghdâdî, 'Abd al-Qâdir . . ., *Khizânat al-Adab*, 4 vols., Bûlâq 1299/1882.

Al-Bâgûrî, v. Ibrâhîm al-Bâgûrî.

Al-Bannânî, v. 'Abd ar-Rahmân al-Bannânî.

Al-Baydâwî, 'Abdallah b. 'Umar, *Anwâr at-Tanzîl wa-Asrâr at-Ta'wîl*, Mustafâ al-Bâbî al-Halabî, Cairo 1344.

Bint as-Shâti', v. 'Â'isha 'Abd ar-Rahmân.

Dalîl al-Kitâb al-Misrî 1972, [Egyptian books in print 1972], Cairo 1972.

Ad-Dardîrî, v. Yahyâ Ahmad ad-Dardîrî.

Darwaza, v. Muhammad 'Izza Darwaza.

Darwîsh al-Gundî, *An-Nazm al-Qur'ânî fî Kashshâf az-Zamakhsharî*, Dâr Nahdat Misr, Cairo 1969.

Dayf, v. Shawqî Dayf.

Ad-Dhahabî, v. Muhammad Husayn ad-Dhahabî.

Ad-Du'alî, Abû al-Aswad, *Dîwân*, ed. 'Abd al-Karîm ad-Dugaylî, Baghdâd 1954.

Fahmî, v. 'Abd al-'Azîz Fahmî.

Fahkr ad-Dîn ar-Râzî, *Mafâtih al-Ghayb*, 6 vols., Cairo 1278/1862.

Al-Fandî, v. Gamâl ad-Dîn al-Fandî.

Farîd Wagdî, v. Muhammad Farîd Wagdî.

Fawda, v. 'Abd ar-Rahîm Fawda.

Al-Fîrûzâbâdî, Abû Tâhir Muhammad b. Ya'qûb, *Tanwîr al-Miqbâs min Tafsîr b. 'Abbâs*, Mustafâ al-Bâbî al-Halabî, Cairo 1951[2].

Gamâl ad-Dîn al-Fandî, *Al-Qur'ân wa-l-'Ilm*, Dâr al-Ma'rifa, Cairo 1968[1].

Gawharî, v. Tantâwî Gawharî.

Al-Ghazâlî, Abû Hâmid . . ., *Gawâhir al-Qur'ân*, Cairo 1329.

——, *Ihyâ 'Ulûm ad-Dîn*, 4 vols., Mustafâ al-Bâbî al-Halabî, Cairo 1939.

Al-Ghazâlî, v. Muhammad al-Ghazâlî.

Al-Ghubâshî, v. 'Abd al-'Azîm Ahmad al-Ghubâshî.

Al-Ghumârî, v. Abû al-Fadl 'Abdallah Muhammad as-Sâdiq al-Ghumârî.

Al-Gundî, v. Anwar al-Gundî.

Al-Guwaynî, v. Mustafâ as-Sâwî al-Guwaynî.

Hâfiz 'Îsâ 'Ammâr, *At-Tafsîr al-Hadîth li-l-Qur'ân al-Karîm*, Mustafâ al-Bâbî al-Halabî, Cairo 1379/1960.

Hamûda, v. 'Abd al-Wahhâb Hamûda.

Hanafî Ahmad, *Mu'gizat al-Qur'ân fî Wasf al-Kâ'inât*, Matb. Lagnat al-Bayân al-'Arabî, Cairo 1373/1954.

——, *At-Tafsîr al-'Ilmî li-l-Âyât al-Kawniyya fî-l-Qur'ân*, Dâr al-Ma'ârif, Cairo 1968[2].

Hasan 'Ulwân, v. Mahmûd Muhammad Hamza.

Hasanayn Muhammad Makhlûf, *Kalimât al-Qur'ân, Tafsîr wa-Bayân*, Mustafâ al-Bâbî al-Halabî, Cairo 1965[6].

Higâzî, v. Muhammad Mahmûd Higâzî.

Hilâl ʿAlî Hilâl, *At-Tafsîr an-Numûdhagî, Tafsîr al-Qurʾân Kamâ Yanbaghî an Yakûn*, Tantâ 1968.

Al-Hûfî, v. Ahmad Muhammad al-Hûfî.

Husayn, v. Muhammad Kâmil Husayn.

Husayn al-Harâwî, *An-Nazariyyât al-ʿIlmiyya fî-l-Qurʾân*, Matb. ar-Risâla, Cairo 1361/1942.

Ibrâhîm al-Abyârî, *Taʾrîkh al-Qurʾân*, Dâr al-Qalam, Cairo 1965.

Ibrâhîm ʿAzzûr, Saʿd Shalabî, ʿAbd al-Fattâh Ismâʿîl Shalabî, *Guzʾ ʿAmmâ wa-Tafsîruh*, Makt. Misr, Cairo n.d.

——, *Guzʾ Qad Samiʿa wa-Tafsîruh*, Makt. Misr, Cairo n.d.

——, *Guzʾ Tabâraka wal-Tafsîruh*, Makt. Misr, Cairo n.d.

Ibrâhîm al-Bâgûrî, *Hâshiyyat .... Ibrâhîm al-Bâgûrî ʿalâ Sharh al-ʿAllâma b. Qâsim al-Ghazzî ʿalâ Matn as-Shaykh Abî Shugâʿ ....*, Mustafâ al-Bâbî al-Halabî, Cairo n.d.

Ibrâhîm Markât (?), *At-Tafsîr al-Mukhtasar, li-l-Madâris al-Ibtidâʾiyya*, Makt. ar-Rashâd, Casablanca n.d. (1970 ?).

Ibrâhîm ar-Râwî ar-Rifâʿî, *Sûr as-Sharîʿa fî Intiqâd Nazariyyât Ahl al-Hayʾa wa-t-Tabîʿa*, Makt. al-ʿArabiyya, Cairo 1342.

ʿIffat Muhammad as-Sharqâwî, *Ittigâhât at-Tafsîr fî Misr fî-l-ʿAsr al-Hadîth*, Matb. al-Kîlânî, Cairo 1972.

Al-Iskandarânî, Muhammad b. Ahmad, *Kashf al-Asrâr an-Nûrâniyya al-Qurʾâniyya fî-mâ yataʿallaq bi-l-Agrâm as-Samâwiyya wa-l-Ardiyya wa-l-Hayawanât wa-n-Nabât wa-l-Gawâhir al-Maʿadaniyya*, 3 vols., Matb. al-Wahbiyya, Cairo 1297.

——, *Tibyân al-Asrâr ar-Rabbâniyya fî-n-Nabât wa-l-Maʿâdin wa-l-Khawâss al-Hayawâniyya*, Damascus 1300/1883.

Ismâʿîl, v. ʿAbd al-ʿAzîz Ismâʿîl.

Ismâʿîl Shalabî, v. Ibrâhîm ʿAzzûr.

Kathîr, ʿImâd ad-Dîn Abû al-Fidâʾ Ismâʿîl b., *Tafsîr al-Qurʾân al-ʿAzîm*, ʿÎsâ al-Bâbî al-Halabî, Cairo n.d.

Khalafallâh, v. Muhammad Ahmad Khalafallâh.

Khaldûn, ʿAbd ar-Rahmân b. Muhammad b., *Muqaddima*, Matb. Mustafâ Muhammad, Cairo n.d.

b. al-Khatîb, *Awdah at-Tafâsîr*, Al-Matb. al-Misriyya[7], Cairo n.d.

Al-Khûlî, v. Amîn al-Khûlî.

Labîb as-Saʿîd, *Al-Gamʿ as-Sawtî al-Awwal li-l-Qurʾân al-Karîm*, Dâr al-Kâtib al-ʿArabî, Cairo 1387/1967.

Lagna min al-ʿUlamâʾ bi-Ishrâf ..... al-Azhar, *At-Tafsîr al-Wasît li-l-Qurʾân al-Karîm*, Cairo 1972.

Magallat al-Azhar, (Issued by the rectorate of the Azhar Mosque), Cairo 1935→).

Magallat as-Shubbân al-Muslimîn, (the periodical of the Moslem Young Men's Association).

Al-Maghribî, v. ʿAbd al-Qâdir al-Maghribî.

Al-Maglis al-Aʿlâ li-s-Shuʾûn al-Islâmiyya, *Al-Muntakhab fî Tafsîr al-Qurʾân al-Karîm*, Cairo 1968.

Magmaʿ al-Lugha al-ʿArabiyya, *Muʿgam Alfâz al-Qurʾân al-Karîm*, Al-Hayʾa al-Misriyya al-ʿÂmma, Cairo 1970[2].

Mahmûd Farag al-ʿUqda, *Tafsîr Guzʾ ʿAmmâ*, Matb. Subayh, Cairo 1966.

Mahmûd Muhammad Hamza, Hasan ʿUlwân, Muhammad Ahmad Barâniq, *Tafsîr al-Qurʾân al-Karîm*, 30 vols., Dâr al-Maʿârif, Cairo 1968[20].

Mahmûd Shalabî, ed., *Tafsîr al-Fâtiha, li-l-Imâm . . . at-Tabarî*, Dâr al-Fikr al-ʿArabî, Cairo 1388/1968.

——, *Tafsîr Âyat al-Kursî . . . li-l-Aʾimma al-Kibâr*: *Al-Fakhr ar-Râzî, b. Kathîr, al-Âlûsî*, Matb. al-ʿÂlamiyya, Cairo 1388/1968.

Mahmûd Shaltût, *Al-Fatâwâ*, Dâr al-Qalam, Cairo n.d.[3].

——, *Manhag al-Qurʾân fî Binâʾ al-Mugtamaʿ*, Dâr al-Kitâb al-ʿArabî, Cairo 1375.

——, *Al-Islâm ʿAqîda wa-Sharîʿa*, Dâr al-Qalam, Cairo 1966[3].

——, *Tafsîr al-Qurʾân al-Karîm, al-Agzâʾ al-ʿAshara al-Ûlâ*, Dâr al-Qalam, Cairo 1966[4].

——, *Min Tawgîhât al-Islâm*, Dâr al-Qalam, Cairo 1966[3].

——, *Min Hudâ al-Qurʾân*, Dâr al-Kâtib al-ʿArabî, Cairo 1968.

——, *Ilâ al-Qurʾân al-Karîm*, Dâr al-Hilâl, Cairo n.d.

Makhlûf, v. Hasanayn Muhammad Makhlûf.

Al-Manfalûtî, v. Mustafâ Lutfî al-Manfalûtî.

Al-Marâghî, v. Ahmad Mustafâ al-Marâghî.

Al-Marâghî, v. Muhammad Mustafâ al-Marâghî.

Muhammad ʿAbdallâh al-Hamsharî, *Sûrat an-Nisâʾ*, Alexandria 1377/1958.

Muhammad ʿAbd al-Munʿim al-Gamâl, *At-Tafsîr al-Farîd li-l-Qurʾân al-Magîd*, Cairo 1971.

Muhammad ʿAbd al-Munʿim Khafâgî, *Tafsîr al-Qurʾân al-Hakîm*, Makt. an-Nagâh, An-Nagaf n.d.[1].

Muhammad ʿAbd ar-Rahmân al-Gudaylî, *Nazarât Hadîtha fî-t-Tafsîr*, Beirouth.

Muhammad ʿAbduh, *Tafsîr Guzʾ ʿAmmâ*, al-Matb. al-Amîriyya, Cairo 1322.

——, *Tafsîr Sûrat al-ʿAsr*, Cairo 1903.

——, [Tafsîr al-Fâtiha], *Fâtihat al-Kitâb, Tafsîr al-Ustâdh al-Imâm . . .*, Kitâb at-Tahrîr, Cairo 1382.

——, *Durûs min al-Qurʾân al-Karîm*, Ed. Tâhir at-Tanâkhî, Dâr al-Hilâl, Cairo n.d.

Muhammad Abû Zuhra, *Al-ʿAqîda al-Islâmiyya*, Cairo 1969.

Muhammad Abû Zayd, *Al-Hidâya wa-l-ʿIrfân fî Tafsîr al-Qurʾân bi-l-Qurʾân*, Mustafâ al-Bâbî al-Halabî, Cairo 1349.

Muhammad Ahmad Barâniq, v. Mahmûd Muhammad Hamza.

Muhammad Ahmad Khalafallâh, *Al-Qurʾân wa-Mushkilât Hayâtinâ al-Muʿâsira*, Makt. al-Anglû al-Misriyya, Cairo 1967.

——, *Al-Fann al-Qasasî fî-l-Qurʾân al-Karîm*, Makt. al-Anglû-al-Misriyya, Cairo 1972[4].

Muhammad ʿAlî as-Sâyis, *Tafsîr Âyât al-Ahkâm*, Matb. Subayh, Cairo 1373/1953.

Muhammad Bâqir al-Muwahhid al-Abtahî, *Al-Madkhal ilâ at-Tafsîr al-Mawdûʿî li-l-Qurʾân al-Karîm*, Matb. al-Âdâb, An-Nagaf 1389/1969.

Muhammad al-Fâdil b. Âshûr, *At-Tafsîr wa-Rigâluh*, Tunis 1966.

Muhammad Farîd Wagdî, *Muqaddimat al-Mushaf al-Mufassar*, Matb. Dâʾirat Maʿârif al-Qarn al-ʿIshrîn, Cairo 1349/1930.

——, *Al-Mushaf al-Mufassar*, Dâr ash-Shaʿb, Cairo n.d.

Muhammad Gamâl ad-Dîn ʿAyyâd, *Buhûth fî Tafsîr al-Qurʾân*, Cairo 1968.

——, *Tafsîr al-Qurʾân, Sûrat al-Muzammil, Tafsîr . . li-l-Muthaqqafîn . . ka-l-Atibbâʾ wa-l-Muhandisîn . .*, Matb. al-Maʿrifa, Cairo 1968.

——, *Tafsîr al-Qurʾân, Sûrat at-Takwîr*, Dâr al-Fikr al-ʿArabî, Cairo 1969.

——, *Buhûth fî Tafsîr al-Qurʾân, Sûrat al-ʿAlaq*, Cairo 1380/1961.

[Muhammad Gamâl ad-Dîn al-Fandî], Muhammad Jamaluddin El-Fandy, *On Cosmic Verses in the Quran*, Cairo 1967.

——, *Min Rawâ'i' al-I'gâz fî-l-Qur'ân al-Karîm*, Al-Maglis al-A'lâ li-s-Shu'ûn al-Islâmiyya, Cairo 1969.

Muhammad Gamâl ad-Dîn al-Qâsimî, *Tafsîr al-Qâsimi, al-Musammâ: Mahâsin at-Ta'wîl*, ed. Muhammad Fu'âd 'Abd al-Bâqî, 'Îsâ al-Bâbî al-Halabî, Cairo 1376/1957.

Muhammad al-Ghazâlî, *Nazarât fî-l-Qur'ân*, Dâr al-Kutub al-Hadîtha, Cairo 1382/1962 [3].

Muhammad Husayn ad-Dhahabî, *At-Tafsîr wa-l-Mufassirûn*, 3 vols., Dâr al-Kutub al-Hadîtha, Cairo 1961-1962.

Muhammad Ismâ'îl Ibrâhîm, *Mu'gam al-Alfâz wa-l-A'lâm al-Qur'âniyya*, Dâr al-Fikr al-'Arabî, Cairo 1969 [2].

Muhammad 'Izza Darwaza, *At-Tafsîr al-Hadîth*, 12 vols., 'Îsâ al-Bâbî al-Halabî, Cairo 1962.

Muhammad Kâmil Daww, *Al-Qur'ân al-Karîm wa-l-'Ulûm al-Hadîtha*, Dâr al-Fikr al-Hadîth, Cairo 1955 [2].

Muhammad Kâmil Husayn, *Ad-Dhikr al-Hakîm*, Makt. an-Nahda al-Misriyya, Cairo 1971.

Muhammad al-Khudarî, *Al-Qawl as-Shâfî fî Tafsîr al-Mu'awwidhatayn*, Matb. at-Tawakkul, Cairo 1367/1948.

Muhammad Mahmûd Higâzî, *At-Tafsîr al-Wâdih*, 30 vols., Matb. al-Istiqlâl, Cairo 1964 [5].

——, *Al-Wahda al-Mawdû'iyya fî-l-Qur'ân al-Karîm*, Dâr al-Kutub al-Hadîtha, Cairo 1970.

Muhammad al-Mubârak 'Abdallâh, *Tafsîr Guz' 'Ammâ*, Makt. Subayh, Cairo n.d.

Muhammad Muhyî ad-Dîn 'Abd al-Hamîd, *Tafsîr a-Qur'ân al-'Azîm, Guz' 'Ammâ*, Matb. Higâzî, Cairo n.d.

Muhammad Mustafâ al-Marâghî, *Bahth fî Targamat al-Qur'ân al-Karîm wa-Ahkâmhâ*, Cairo 1936.

——, *Ad-Durûs ad-Dîniyya*, Matb. al-Azhar, Cairo 1356-64.

Muhammad Ragab al-Bayyûmî, *Khutuwât at-Tafsîr al-Bayânî li-l-Qur'ân al-Karîm*, Cairo 1971.

——, "At-tafsîr al-bayânî li-l-Qur'ân al-Karîm", *Qâfilat az-Zayt*, xx, 3, 3 (1972).

Muhammad Rashîd Ridâ, *Targamat al-Qur'ân wa-mâ fîhâ min Mafâsid wa-Munâfât al-Islâm*, Cairo 1925.

——, *Tafsîr al-Qur'ân al-Hakîm al-Mushtahir bi-Tafsîr al-Manâr*, 12 vols., Cairo 1954 [4]-1961.

——, *Tafsîr al-Fâtiha wa-6 Suwar min Khawâtîm al-Qur'ân*, Matb. al-Manâr, Cairo 1367 [2].

——, *Tafsîr Sûrat Yûsuf*, Matb. al-Manâr, Cairo 1355/1936.

Muhammad as-Sâdiq 'Argûn, *Al-Qur'ân al-'Azîm, Hidâyatuh wa-I'gâzuh fî-Aqwâl al-Mufassirîn*, Makt. al-Kulliyyât al-Azhariyya, Cairo 1966.

Muhammad Siddîq Hasan Khân, *Nayl al-Marâm min Tafsîr Âyât al-Ahkâm*, Makt. at-Tigâriyya al-Kubrâ, Cairo 1383/1963 [3].

[Muhammad] Siddîq Hasan Khân, *Al-Maw'iza al-Hasana bi-mâ Yukhtab fî Shuhûr as-Sana*, Beirouth n.d.

Muhammad Subayh, *Bahth Gadîd 'an al-Qur'ân*, Dâr at-Thaqâfa al-'Âmma, Cairo 1386/1966 [6].

Muhammad Sulaymân, *Hadath al-Ahdâth fî-l-Islâm, al-Iqdâm 'alâ Targamat al-Qur'ân*, Garîdat Misr al-Hurra, Cairo 1355 [2].

Muhammad at-Tâhir b. 'Âshûr, *Tafsîr at-Tahrîr wa-t-Tanwîr*, 'Îsâ al-Bâbî al-Halabî, Cairo 1384/1964.

Muhammad Tawfîq Sidqî, *Ad-Dîn fî Nazar al-ʿAql as-Sahîh*, Cairo 1323; 1346[2].

——, *Nazra fî Kutub al-ʿAhd al-Gadîd*, Cairo 1331 [1913].

——, *Durûs Sunan al-Kâʾinât*, Cairo 1354[3].

Muhammad Tawfîq ʿUbayd, *Tafsîr Guzʾ ʿAmmâ*, al-Maktaba al-ʿArabiyya, Damascus 1383/1964[5]

Muhammad Yûsuf Mûsâ, *Al-Qurʾân wa-l-Falsafa*, Dâr al-Maʿârif, Cairo 1966.

Muhsin ʿAbd al-Hamîd, *Al-Âlûsî Mufassir[an]*, Baghdad 1968.

Mustafâ Lutfî al-Manfalûtî, *An-Nazarât*, Matb. al-Maʿârif, Cairo 1910.

Mustafâ Mahmûd, *Al-Qurʾân, Muhâwala li-Fahm ʿAsrî li-l-Qurʾân*, Rûz al-Yûsuf, Cairo n.d. [1970].

Mustafâ as-Saqqâ, *Al-Wagîz fî Tafsîr al-Kitâb al-ʿAzîz*, Mustafâ al-Bâbî al-Halabî, Cairo 1387/1967.

Mustafâ as-Sâwî al-Guwaynî, *Minhag az-Zamakhsharî fî Tafsîr al-Qurʾân wa-Bayân Iʿgâzih*, Dâr al-Maʿârif, Cairo 196[2].

Mustafâ Zayd, *Sûrat al-Anfâl, ʿArd wa Tafsîr*, Dâr al-Fikr al-ʿArabî, Cairo 1377/1957[3].

——, *An-Naskh fî-l-Qurʾân al-Karîm, Dirâsa Tashrîʿiyya Taʾrîkhiyya Naqdiyya*, Dâr al-Fikr al-ʿArabî, Cairo 1383/1963.

——, *Dirâsât fî-t-Tafsîr*, Dâr al-Fikr al-ʿArabî, Cairo 1967/68.

Al-Nasafî, Abû al-Barakât ʿAbdallâh b. Ahmad b. Mahmûd, *Tafsîr al-Nasafî*, ʿÎsa al-Bâbî al-Halabî, Cairo n.d.

Nawfal, v. ʿAbd ar-Razzâq Nawfal.

Niʿmat Sidqî, *Muʿgizat al-Qurʾân*, Cairo 1971.

Nûr al-Islâm, (Issued by the rectorate of the Azhar, predecessor of Magallat al-Azhar). Cairo 1930-35.

Qâsim Amîn, *Tahrîr al-Marʾa*, Cairo 1899.

Qâsim al-Qaysî, *Taʾrîkh at-Tafsîr*, Matb. al-Magmaʿ al-ʿIlmî al-ʿIrâqî, n.p., 1966.

Al-Qâsimî, v. Muhammad Gamâl ad-Dîn al-Qâsimi.

b. Qayyim al-Gawziyya, *At-Tibyân fî Aqsâm al-Qurʾân*, ed. Tâhâ Yûsuf Shahîn, Dâr at-Tibâʿa al-Muhammadiyya, Cairo 1388/1968.

Qutb, v. Sayyid Qutb.

Ramzî Naʿnâʿa, *Bidaʿ at-Tafâsîr, fî-l-Mâdî wa-l-Hâdir*, Wizârat al-Awqâf, Amman 1970.

Rashîd Ridâ, v. Muhammad Rashîd Ridâ.

Ar-Râzî, v. Fakhr ad-Dîn ar-Râzî.

Ridâ, v. Muhammad Rashîd Ridâ.

Ar-Rifâʿî, v. Ibrâhîm ar-Râwî ar-Rifâʿî.

Saʿd Shalabî, v. Ibrâhîm ʿAzzûr.

Salâh ad-Dîn Khattâb, *Al-Gânib al-ʿIlmî fî-l-Qurʾân*, Cairo 1970.

Salâma, Abû al-Qâsim Hibat Allâh b., *An-Nâsikh wa-l-Mansûkh*, Mustafâ al-Bâbî al-Halabî, Cairo 1379/1960.

Sarkis, Y. A., *Muʿgam al-Matbûʿât . . . .*, 2 vols., Cairo 1928.

Sayyid Qutb, *At-Taswîr al-Fannî fî-l-Qurʾân*, Dâr al-Maʿârif, Cairo 1959.

——, *Fî Zilâl al-Qurʾân*, 30 vols., Beirouth n.d.[4].

——, *Mashâhid al-Qiyâma fî-l-Qurʾân*, Dâr al-Maʿârif, Cairo n.d.[2].

Shakîb Arslân, *Al-Irtisâmât al-Litâf . . .*, Cairo 1350/1931.

Shalabî, v. Mahmûd Shalabî.

Shaltût, v. Mahmûd Shaltût.

As-Sharabâsî, v. Ahmad as-Sharabâsî.

As-Sharqâwî, v. ʿIffat Muhammad as-Sharqâwî.

Shawqî Dayf, *Sûrat ar-Rahmân wa-Suwar Qisâr*, Dâr al-Maʿârif, Cairo 1971.

Shihâta, v. ʿAbdallah Mahmûd Shihâta.

Siddîq Hasan Khân, v. Muhammad Siddîq Hasan Khân.

Sidqî, v. Muhammad Tawfîq Sidqî.

As-Sigistânî, Abu Bakr, *Nuzhat al-Qulûb fî Tafsîr Gharîb al-Qurʾân*, ed. Mustafâ ʿInânî, Cairo 1936.

——, *Nuzhat al-Qulûb fî Tafsîr Gharîb al-Qurʾân*, ed. ʿAbd al-Halîm Basyûnî, Cairo n.d.

As-Subkî, v. ʿAbd al-Latîf as-Subkî.

As-Suyûtî, Galâl ad-Dîn, *Al-Itqân fî ʿUlûm al-Qurʾân*, Mustafâ al-Bâbî al-Halabî, Cairo 1951[3].

At-Tabarî, Muhammad b. Garîr, *Gâmiʿ al-Bayân . . .*, Mustafâ al-Bâbî al-Halabî, Cairo 1954.

Tafsîr al-Fâtiha, v. Muhammad ʿAbduh.

Tafsîr Gharîb al-Qurʾân, (An.), Tantâ n.d.

Tafsîr al-Manâr, v. Muhammad Rashîd Ridâ.

Tâhâ ʿAbd al-Barr, *Mudhakkira fî-t-Tafsîr*, Matb. al-ʿUlûm, Cairo 1353/1935[2].

Tantâwî Gawharî, *Al-Gawâhir fî Tafsîr al-Qurʾân, al-Mushtamil ʿalâ ʿAgâʾib Badâʾiʿ al-Mukawwanât wa-Gharâʾib al-Âyât al-Bâhirât*, 26 vols., Mustafâ al-Bâbî al-Halabî, Cairo 1350[2].

——, *Al-Qurʾân wa-l-ʿUlûm al-ʿAsriyya*, Mustafâ al-Bâbî al-Halabî, Cairo 1371/1951[2].

"Taqrîr al-Lagna al-Azhariyya . . ." [on Abû Zayd], *Nûr al-Islâm*, ii, 163-206; 249-281. Cairo 1350.

Taymiyya, Taqî ad-Dîn b., *Muqaddima fî Usûl at-Tafsîr*, Matb. at-Taraqqî, Damascus 1936.

ʿUlaysh, v. ʿAbdallâh Muhammad Ahmad Muhammad ʿUlaysh.

ʿUthmân Amîn, *Râʾid al-Fikr al-Misrî, al-Imâm Muhammad ʿAbduh*, Makt. al-Anglû al-Misriyya, Cairo 1965[2].

Wagdî, v. Muhammad Farîd Wagdî.

Al-Wâhidî, Abû al-Hasan ʿAlî b. Ahmad, an-Nîsâbûrî, *Asbâb an-Nuzûl*, Mustafâ al-Bâbî al-Halabî, Cairo 1379/1959.

Wizârat al-Awqâf, *Zâd al-Khatîb*, Cairo 1964 [a collection of Khutbaʾs].

Yahyâ Ahmad ad-Dardîrî, *Makânat al-ʿIlm fî-l-Qurʾân, Daʿwat al-Islâm ilâ-l-ʿIlm . . . wa-Âthâr Dhâlik fî-l-Madaniyya al-Gharbiyya*, Matb. as-Salafiyya, Cairo 1364.

Az-Zamakhsharî, Gâr Allâh Mahmûd b. ʿUmar, *Al-Kashshâf ʿan Haqâʾiq at-Tanzîl wa-ʿUyûn al-Aqâwîl*, 4 vols., Mustafâ al-Bâbî al-Halabî, Cairo 1966.

Az-Zangânî, v. Abû ʿAbdallâh az-Zangânî.

INDEXES

SUBJECTS

REFERENCES TO THE KORAN

NAMES

NEDERLANDSE SAMENVATTING

De exegese van de Koran en de exegese van de Bijbel zijn om twee redenen moeilijk vergelijkbaar. De Koran neemt in de Islam een geheel andere plaats in dan de Bijbel in het Christendom, omdat de Koran door de Moslims wordt beschouwd als het ongeschapen Woord van God, ongeveer zoals Christenen Jezus van Nazareth als de Zoon van God beschouwen. Maar dit is niet het enige verschil: bij het Jodendom en het Christendom heeft de gemeente der gelovigen in een geleidelijk verlopend proces zelf bepaald welke teksten wel en welke teksten niet in de canon van de Heilige Schrift zouden worden opgenomen. Pas toen de canon definitief gesloten was, ontstond op grote schaal behoefte aan uitleg van de heilige teksten. De Moslimse gemeente, daarentegen, werd bij de dood van de Profeet in 632 A.D. geconfronteerd met de noodzaak onmiddellijk de via Mohammed tot hun gekomen heilige teksten te verklaren, uit te leggen en toe te passen. Er was na de dood van Mohammed, uiteraard, geen periode waarin men nog kon hopen op ,,aanvullende'' openbaringen, en waarin tegelijkertijd reeds met de uitleg van het voorhanden zijnde materiaal kon worden begonnen. Dit verklaart wellicht dat vanaf het begin de exegese van de Koran een gekunstelde en schoolse indruk maakt.

Er heeft onder orientalisten altijd een ruime belangstelling voor de Moslimse Koranexegese bestaan. De grote hoeveelheden Korankommentaren die sinds het begin van deze eeuw in Egypte gepubliceerd zijn en die niet in de Westerse publicaties over Koranexegese (die van I. Goldziher, J. Jomier en J. M. S. Baljon) genoemd worden, rechtvaardigen wellicht onze nadere aandacht voor dit onderwerp.

De inhoud van de moderne Egyptische Korankommentaren valt uiteen in opmerkingen over de filologie van de Koran; in opmerkingen over de Koran en natuurlijke historie; en in opmerkingen over de Koran en het dagelijks leven van de Moslims. Men zou kunnen zeggen dat de moderne Egyptische Korankommentaren drie aspekten hebben: een natuur-historisch aspekt, een filologisch aspekt en een praktisch aspekt. Het zou minder juist zijn te zeggen dat er sprake is van drie ,,tendenties'' in de moderne Koranexegese indien tenminste daarmee bedoeld zou worden dat de massa van kommentaren overeenkomstig deze drie tendenties in drie groepen verdeeld zou kunnen worden, aangezien de inhoud van elke kommentaar van min of meer gemengde aard is.

Misschien is het onvermijdelijk dat een kommentaar op een heilige tekst deze drie kanten heeft: de „letterlijke" betekenis van de tekst (filologische exegese), de betekenis van de tekst voor het handelen van de mens (praktische exegese), en de betekenis van de tekst voor de kennis van de mens („wetenschappelijke" exegese, *tafsîr 'ilmî*). Wellicht is het mogelijk op een dergelijke wijze ook de oudere kommentaren te analyseren. Hoe het ook zij, de kommentaren die sinds Mohammed Abduh (1848/9-1905) zijn geproduceerd, bezitten deze drie aspekten.

Er is geen Chinese muur tussen de oude en de nieuwe kommentaren. De een is vaak moeilijk te begrijpen zonder de ander, en Egyptenaren die vandaag de dag besluiten hun aandacht aan Koranexegese te geven, bestuderen beide soorten kommentaren gezamenlijk. Het belangrijkste verschil lijkt te zijn dat de „klassieke" kommentaren zijn geschreven in een tijd dat wie lezen kon eigenlijk altijd een theologische training had genoten, terwijl de moderne kommentaren zich (vaak expliciet) richten tot een publiek van geletterden die buiten de Moskee om hebben leren lezen en schrijven. Desalniettemin zijn vorm en inhoud van moderne kommentaren vaak verrassend traditioneel.

Het is opvallend dat Moslims bij de „wetenschappelijke" exegese gebruik maken van de Westerse natuurwetenschappen, zij het op een niveau waarbij wellicht beter gesproken kan worden van elementaire „natuurlijke historie". In het Jodendom en het Christendom is daarentegen de tekst van de Heilige schrift vaak benut om historische wetenschap gewaar te worden: de datum van de val van een vijandig rijk kon, zo meenden sommige Joden en Christenen vaak, uit de schrift afgeleid worden. Dit soort „historische" exegese is bij de Moslims nagenoeg onbekend.

De Moslimse filologische exegese kan nooit uitgaan van het in bepaalde Christelijke kringen zo populaire *e mente auctoris* principe, omdat Moslims geloven dat God de „auteur" van de Koran is. Nu wordt het *e mente auctoris* principe vooral destruktief gebruikt: een bepaalde uitleg die om de een of andere reden onwelkom is wordt verworpen omdat bijvoorbeeld de evangelist Lukas, in zijn tijd, deze niet bedoeld kan hebben. Het feit dat het de mens niet wel mogelijk is te oordelen over wat een almachtig

God wel of niet kan bedoelen, maakt het *e mente auctoris* principe weinig geschikt als „destruktieve" exegetische richtlijn voor Moslimse Koranuitleggers. Desalniettemin is er een equivalent van dit principe te vinden bij de moderne Moslimse Koranexegeten: velen hunner zijn namelijk van mening dat de Koran allereerst verstaan moet worden zoals de eerste Moslims in Mekka en Medina hem verstaan hebben, en dat een uitleg die in dit milieu niet past, niet legitiem is.

Tenslotte is het opvallend dat de Moslimse filologische Koranexegese een zekere gelaagdheid vertoont. De eerste laag, die van de bestudering van de precieze betekenis van de afzonderlijke woorden van de Koran, bestond al ten tijde van Ibn 'Abbâs (zevende eeuw A.D.); de tweede laag, de bestudering van de syntaxis van de Koran, beginnend in het werk van Abû 'Ubayda (negende eeuw A.D.), bereikt zijn hoogtepunt in het werk van Az-Zamakhsharî (twaalfde eeuw A.D.). Weinig uit deze „lagen" is verloren gegaan. In de modernste kommentaren zijn nog duidelijk sporen van het werk van Ibn 'Abbâs, Abû 'Ubayda en Az-Zamakhsharî aanwezig.

De praktische exegese van de Koran beslaat (nog steeds) het gehele leven van de Moslim in deze wereld. Niet alleen de „devotie" (vasten, gebed, pelgrimage, enz.) maar ook zaken als tweedracht in de gemeente en de seculiere rechtspraak (vooral familierecht en strafrecht) komen in aanmerking voor bespreking in Korankommentaren. Hierbij moet men wel bedenken dat de discussie, voorzover niet bestaand uit stichtelijke algemeenheden, vaak slechts in schijn over de Koran en diens juiste interpretatie gaat. Meestal is de mate waarin Westerse invloed op leer en leven toegelaten mag worden het werkelijke onderwerp van het debat.

ISBN 90 04 04009 9